Local Voices, National Issues

Michigan Monograph Series in Japanese Studies
Number 31

Center for Japanese Studies
The University of Michigan

Local Voices, National Issues

The Impact of Local Initiative in
Japanese Policy-Making

Edited by Sheila A. Smith

Ann Arbor   2000
Center for Japanese Studies
The University of Michigan

Published by the Center for Japanese Studies, The University of Michigan
202 S Thayer St., Ann Arbor, MI 48104-1608

Library of Congress Cataloging-in-Publication Data

Local voices, national issues : the impact of local initiative in Japanese
policy-making / edited by Sheila A. Smith.
     p. cm. — (Michigan monograph series in Japanese studies ; no. 31)
  Includes bibliographical references and index.
  ISBN 0-939512-04-1 (cloth : alk. paper)
    1. Central-local government relations—Japan. 2. Local government—
Japan. I. Smith, Sheila A., 1959- II. Series.

JS7373.A3 L63   2000
320.8'0952—dc21
                                                    99-462352

This book was set in Berkeley Oldstyle Book.

Jacket design by Seiko Semones

This publication meets the ANSI/NISO Standards for Permanence of Paper for
Publications and Documents in Libraries and Archives (Z39.48-1992).

Printed in the United States of America

Contents

Preface

This book began as a conversation between two graduate students talking through their dissertations. One was working on Japanese security planning, the other on the impact of Japan's consumer movement and product liability. No two policy issues could have seemed so unrelated to each other, but as the conversation progressed, it was clear that we shared similar questions about the intersection between national policy-making and local political activism in Japan. Moving on from our dissertations, Patricia Maclachlan and I both turned our attention to cases of local politics and policy-making. I was struck by the outburst of protest in Okinawa Prefecture against the U.S. military bases and the governor's effort to curtail Japan's security cooperation with the United States in the wake of the cold war. Patricia Maclachlan found that many of the patterns of citizen activism in consumer affairs were being demonstrated in local efforts to pass information disclosure ordinances. Both of these cases engaged national attention in Japan and, in different ways, forced the central government to contend with policy initiatives that emanated from outside of Tokyo's corridors of power. We were drawn to the energy of local actors, and we wondered whether or not this energy could also be found in other issue areas.

The question of how successful local actors were in articulating their interests in the national policy-making process was an intriguing one. Were local actors becoming more important in shaping national priorities? Were these exceptional instances of local activism, or did they suggest the potential for a transformation in the balance of power between localities and the national government in Japan? These simple questions prompted a panel discussion at the 1998 Association for Asian Studies Annual Meetings, on "Local Initiative in Japanese Policy-making," where we were joined by two other scholars who had conducted extensive research on policy issues at the local level of Japanese politics. Ted

Gilman had looked carefully at economic development planning in Kyushu to see how successful local governments and their constituents were in harnessing Tokyo's resources to revitalize local communities. Katherine Tegtmeyer Pak had completed her dissertation on how local governments and nongovernmental actors were contending with the influx of foreign workers into their communities and how national immigration and social welfare policies affected local efforts to accommodate these new participants in Japanese society.

Our common task was to think about the ways local groups, broadly conceived, attempt to influence national policy-making. Since each of the authors had done extensive field research on their respective topics and had pursued their own projects with rather different overarching questions, we did not seek to shape our comparison beyond this basic inquiry. To help us frame our conversation, however, we asked Ellis Krauss to place our research efforts in the context of postwar studies of local politics in Japan. As Krauss points out, much of recent political science research on Japan has focused on national governance and the policy-making institutions in Tokyo. This tendency is partly a result of the growing interest in the U.S. on how policy-making within Japan will affect the rest of the world. As Krauss notes, however, interest in local politics in Japan resulted in two previous "waves" of scholarship, both of which were interested in how Japanese citizens expanded their participation in the democratic process. These past studies of local politics have highlighted specific social movements that challenged national priorities, and specific moments of intensified local activism within Japanese postwar politics. In contrast, we find in our comparison across issues that citizens and local governments have had quite divergent experiences in making their voices heard at the national level of policy-making.

As our "conversation" continued, we saw that our focus on issues captured a rather complex process of local-national negotiation. New questions emerged. When do localities resist national priorities? How effective are local governments and local citizens' groups in changing, or even helping to establish, these priorities? Can local actors initiate new policies, or are they ultimately destined to accept the policy goals established in Tokyo? When interests clash, how much latitude do local actors have in stopping the national government from imposing unwelcome policies? As the chapters that follow reveal, there are both new opportunities for localities to craft new policy agendas and continuing barriers to changing national priorities once they are defined.

While our conclusions on the ability of local political actors to influence the center may differ, we shared two common objectives. First, we all felt that it was necessary to move away from the center of Japanese politics to gain a better view of national policy-making in Japan. Patricia Maclachlan and Katherine Tegtmeyer Pak did not limit their attention to the national political institutions that are so often credited with producing Japan's policies. Instead they sought out the citizens' groups and nongovernmental organizations that want access to the process. In both cases, these groups managed to transform the way in which policy is made, if not always to get all of the policy changes they desired. In calling for information disclosure ordinances, citizens forced local bureaucrats to come "clean" in responding to requests for information. Ultimately, the cascade of local successes put pressure on the national government to contend with the call for information disclosure at the national level. In the case of foreign workers, the mobilization of advocacy groups representing those left out of the social welfare web crafted by the national bureaucracy has transformed the policy-making process at the local level. As Tegtmeyer Pak points out, these nongovernmental groups give voice to an otherwise silenced constituency and provide foreign residents in Japan with new avenues of access to social support.

Both Ted Gilman's study of economic redevelopment in Kyushu and my study of the U.S. military bases in Okinawa took us quite literally far from the center of Japan. By moving out into regions distant from the day-to-day workings of Japan's national government, our cases also helped to shed some light on how geographic and cultural distance from the urban metropolitan concerns of Tokyo residents affects citizen perspectives on policy-making. The burden of explaining local circumstance, and of making sure these peripheral communities are not forgotten, is on local officials. Yet geographic distance did not weaken the links between local officials and the national bureaucracies responsible for distributing resources. While Omuta's local policy elite considered what kinds of new projects might attract national government funding, Okinawa's prefectural government plotted ways of decreasing their citizen's dependence on national subsidies. Public officials must mediate between resource-rich Tokyo and their own economically deprived regions. However, the quiet, day-to-day negotiations between Omuta and Tokyo over economic development planning provided a stark contrast to the upheaval that resulted in the more public and contentious attempt to renegotiate the compact between Okinawa Prefecture and the national government over the U.S. military bases.

Our second common concern was with the consumers of Japanese policy-making. In each of the chapters, there is a common underlying question about how the consumers of policy in Japan are incorporated in the policy-making process. Public policy is by its very nature designed to meet the needs of citizens. The four issue areas considered offer divergent styles of negotiation between public officials and citizens. Moreover, the degree to which Japanese citizens demanded a greater role in the policy-making process also varied. Patricia Steinhoff's overview of the four cases in the concluding chapter allows us to take a step back from the specifics of each study to consider anew the relationship between Japan's "public officials" and the citizens they are obligated to represent. By placing our individual cases in the broader context of the evolution of state-society relations in Japan, Steinhoff identifies some of the more successful avenues for articulating citizen interest as well as the factors that hindered greater voice in the policy-making produced.

In combining our efforts to understand the nexus of local-national relations in Japan, we hope to offer a variety of glimpses into the way in which democracy is practiced there. These chapters present a rich array of political interactions, some contentious, some not. As a whole, this volume seeks to shed greater light on the ways in which members of Japanese society seek to make their voices heard within the political process. We also hope that we have succeeded in sharpening the focus on the faces that populate the day-to-day wrangle of Japanese politics—the often invisible Japanese citizen, bureaucrat, local politician, and social activist, who seeks to ensure that local interests are heard within the national institutions of government. As national politicians shift party affiliations and create new coalitions of majority power, it is tempting to become focused on the personalities and the rivalries in the spotlight in Tokyo. As the following chapters suggest, however, it is equally important that we continue to direct our gaze beyond Tokyo if we wish to expand our understanding of the dynamics of Japanese politics and society. Outside of the narrow confines of Kasumigaseki and Nagatachō are a host of individuals, groups, and leaders who are also participants and agents of change in Japanese politics.

This book is the product of sustained and multiple "conversations" between the contributors and others within the field who provided feedback and guidance. The authors have noted their respective debts in their chapters. The project could not have succeeded, however, without the support of several key individuals. Particular gratitude is due to Patricia Steinhoff, who not only added the perspective of a sociologist to the project but also shepherded it through to its ultimate publication. She commented on individual drafts and gave considerably of her expertise and time well after her responsibilities as "discussant" were over. John Campbell of the University of Michigan was also an enthusiastic supporter, and our editor at the Center for Japanese Studies, Bruce Willoughby, pa-tiently and expertly guided the book to publication. All contributors were graceful—even cheerful—in their efforts to meet deadlines, even in the face of new jobs, new families, and trans-Pacific travels. I could not have asked for a better group of colleagues. I would also like to thank Alexis Sentell for her assistance with the index. Last but not least, I would like to return to the beginning, and thank my partner throughout this "conversa-tion," Patricia Maclachlan.

Sheila A. Smith
January 2000

Local Politics In Japan: Welcoming the Third Wave

Ellis S. Krauss

More than many social scientists would like to admit, the amount of scholarship produced on a given subject is often the result of the amount of attention a subject is receiving in current affairs. The greater the salience of an issue, and the fewer the scholars working in a field, the higher the proportion of research that will be devoted to that particular subject in the field. Especially given the small number of scholars who are experts on Japan in the United States, this often results in cycles, or waves, of research on a particular topic.

The history of scholarship on local politics and center-local relations in Japan is a classic illustration of this formula. There have been three cycles of interest in these subjects. Each of these waves has followed arguably some of the most important periods of major change in Japanese politics in the postwar period, and coincided with a particular scholarly generation's entrance into the field. The first was the fundamental reforms to local government of the American Occupation of Japan, experience in which stimulated the founder of this subfield in the United States; the second was the late 1960s and early 1970s when, for the first time, local politics was the focal point of conflict between left and right, and the site of an unprecedented grass-roots movement; the final "wave" is the current revitalized interest in local affairs among the young scholars represented in the articles that follow.

The American field of local politics in Japan begins literally with one man, Kurt Steiner, back in the 1950s. Steiner, the *doyen* of this field, had himself participated in the reorganization of local government under the Occupation as a young army officer. His Ph.D. dissertation at Stanford several years later was turned into the book, *Local Government in Japan*.[1] This voluminous classic described the complications and impli-

---

1. Kurt Steiner, *Local Government in Japan* (Stanford: Stanford University Press, 1965).

cations of Japan's complex system of center-local relations, a system far different than that found in the United States. His work to this day remains a very useful compendium and reference for those interested in local government, politics, and center-local relations in Japan.

Although anthropologists naturally often conducted ethnographic research at the local level, other than Steiner few of the very small number of political scientists of Japan in the 1950s and 1960s, many of whom also had experience in the Occupation or in the military thereafter, paid much attention to it.[2] The 1960 treaty crisis, the development of political parties and the initiation of some new ones, and interpretations of Japan's "modernization" occupied center stage in a very small theater.

All this changed with the early 1970s, as Japan itself underwent a major political transformation. Contemporaneous with this transformation was the entry of a new generation of political scientists specializing on Japan. This generation, trained in systematic social science in the burgeoning American universities of the mid- to late-1960s, were attracted to the field of local politics for their dissertation research, or for their first research after their dissertation research, by the momentous issues of the late 1960s to early 1970s: pollution, citizens' direct participation in politics, and local autonomy.[3]

After a generation of unparalleled industrial growth unfettered by concern or attention to its pernicious side effects, Japan's environment was one of, if not the, most polluted on earth. I recall that during my years of dissertation research in Tokyo, school children were collapsing in school yards from noxious air inversion, and I remember reading about one street corner in Tokyo where the traffic policeman had to take a periodic break from directing traffic to breathe oxygen because the air was so full of lead fumes.

Stimulated by four court cases initiated by victims of pollution in specific localities, and tremendous new media attention to the problem of the environment, citizens' (also called residents') movements sprung up in many locales throughout Japan to prevent the location of polluting industrial facilities in their areas. These movements and their consequences were unique in several respects.

2. Yasumasa Kuroda's *Reed Town, Japan: A Study in Community Power Structure and Political Change* (Honolulu: University of Hawaii Press, 1974) is an exception. Based on early 1960s field research, it was an attempt to apply the traditional community power theories of American political science to Japan.

3. Descriptions of the development and importance of these issues can be found in Kurt Steiner, Ellis S. Krauss, and Scott C. Flanagan, eds., *Political Opposition and Local Politics in Japan* (Princeton: Princeton University Press, 1980).

First, the tradition of democratic civic action did not have a long history in Japan, unlike in the United States. Accustomed to their status as subjects of the emperor from before the war, the Japanese viewed the American Occupation's civic lessons about the participatory rights of democratic citizens as largely abstract textbook concepts. Although Japanese exercised their right to vote in proportions higher than in the United States and joined voluntary associations in great numbers after the war, most Japanese confined their direct participation to these acts. The mass mobilization of ordinary citizens who perceived a threat to democracy during the 1960 U.S.-Japan treaty crisis was an important exception, and one that set a precedent for the citizens' movements against pollution. These movements were seen at the time as nothing less than the cause and manifestation of a transformation from a passive to active political citizenry.

Second, that this direct action and involvement of citizens was taking place at the local level, normally an arena dominated by conservative local governments and conservative norms and organizations, was even more surprising.

Third, these movements cut across traditional cleavages and attracted citizens of all socioeconomic classes and political persuasions.

Fourth, although they often allied themselves with leftist parties or groups, they strove to be genuinely independent of conventional political groupings and avoided being co-opted by them.

Fifth, jumping on the bandwagon of the public's growing revulsion against industrial pollution that had been brought about by the conservative center's policies, as well as the dearth of social welfare and civilized infrastructure that were also the consequences of those policies, the socialist and communist parties and their candidates picked up these issues and rode to victory in local elections, especially for mayor or governor, the only directly elected posts in the Japanese political system. The conservative ruling Liberal Democratic Party belatedly got the message that was being sent by voters and in 1970 passed fourteen stringent anti-pollution control bills in the National Diet, but not before over 40% of Japanese citizens by the early-mid-1970s were living under leftist local executives.

Sixth, many of these executives carried out innovative policies to respond to residents' desire for greater services and safety, and touted the need for the national government to provide more autonomy to the locales and for the locales to provide more opportunity for direct citizen input into policies. In a political system in which the national government raised two-thirds of the tax revenue but the local governments ac-

counted for two-thirds of government spending (with the difference being made up by transfers from the central government to the locales),
where the national government could delegate and supervise the implementation of many policies to the local governments, and where the central bureaucracy was reputedly extremely powerful in policy-making, a
program of more local autonomy and citizen input represented a major
departure from existing political reality and consciousness in Japan.

For American graduate students and young assistant and associate professors, these unprecedented changes in Japanese politics provided
an exciting opportunity to conduct research on the causes, operation, and
consequences of this transformation. In the process they discovered Kurt
Steiner's pioneering study and the work of Japanese experts on local politics and public administration like Muramatsu Michio of Kyoto University. The titles of the books and articles this generation produced are indicative of this profound new interest stimulated by these changes in
Japan: James W. White and Frank Munger's *Social Change and Community Politics in Urban Japan;*[4] Margaret McKean's *Environmental Protest
and Citizen Politics in Japan;*[5] Richard Samuels's *The Politics of Regional
Policy in Japan: Localities Incorporated?;*[6] and Kurt Steiner's edited volume with Scott Flanagan and me, *Political Opposition and Local Politics
in Japan.*[7] The latter volume contained several articles: Scott Flanagan's
and Terry MacDougall's on local elections and election behavior, Gary
Allinson's study of opposition politics in a suburb; Jack G. Lewis's case
study of a citizens' movement in Mishima city and Meg McKean's on citizens' movements as a socialization experience; Ron Aqua's analysis of
policy change in Japanese cities; my own on leftist government in Kyoto
Prefecture and (with Bradford Simcock) on citizens' movements against
pollution; as well as Steiner's articles placing the study of local politics
in Japan into a theoretical context and analyzing center-local relations
and public policy under leftist local governments.[8]

4. James W. White and Frank Munger, *Social Change and Community Politics in Urban
Japan* (Chapel Hill: Institute for Research in Social Science, 1976).
5. Margaret McKean, *Environmental Protest and Citizen Politics in Japan* (Berkeley: University of California Press, 1981)
6. Richard J. Samuels, *The Politics of Regional Policy in Japan: Localities Incorporated?*
(Princeton: Princeton University Press, 1983).
7. Steiner, Krauss, and Flanagan., *Political Opposition and Local Politics in Japan.*
8. These articles' titles are, respectively: "Political Socialization Through Citizens' Movements"; "Electoral Change in Japan: An Overview" and "National and Local Voting
Trends: Cross-Level Linkages and Correlates of Change"; "Political Opposition and Big
City Elections in Japan, 1947–1975"; "Opposition in the Suburbs"; "Citizens' Movements:
The Growth and Impact of Environmental Protest in Japan" and "Opposition in Power:

All of this work represented a significant proportion of the research time, energy, attention, and publications of political scientists of Japan during the decade from 1970 to 1980. A final contribution appeared in the mid-1980s, Steven R. Reed's *Japanese Prefectures and Policymaking*.[9] The focus of all this effort was on whether, how, and why this social and political change was transforming Japanese politics, and on why such innovative politics and policy could occur within the context of the seemingly perennial and centralized rule of the conservatives at the national level, and with what effects.

And then, during the following decade or more from the mid-1980s to the present, local politics virtually disappeared from the radar scope of the field, as the wave of change subsided, and the conservatives reconsolidated their hold at both the center and local levels (albeit in a different form). Many of the young scholars who had carried out this prolific research, now increasingly less fitting of the adjective "young," instead turned or returned their attention to subjects such as political economy or voting behavior. These were themes that were more consonant with both the trends within the general field of political science and the salient issues in the current development of Japanese politics.

And now we come to the third wave, the work of the young scholars whose articles follow. Unlike the previous waves, the catalyst to the sudden rise in work on local affairs among so many young political scientists is not quite as obvious: there has been no major restructuring of center-local relations as under the Occupation, and no recent, widespread local movements or shifts in political power at the local level as a generation ago. Nevertheless, even if more indirectly than previous waves, these scholars' interest in local politics has also been stimulated and influenced by major transformations in Japan's political environment.

The first stimulus has been the end of the cold war and increasing internationalization among nations that has led, in democratic nations as well as in former Communist ones, to more attention to levels beyond and below the nation-state, and sometimes to the relationship between the international and local levels. This is most obvious in two of the articles that follow, Katherine Tegtmeyer Pak's study of nongov-

---

The Development and Maintenance of Leftist Government in Kyoto Prefecture"; "Political Choice and Policy Change in Medium-Sized Japanese Cities, 1962–1974"; "Toward a Framework for the Study of Local Opposition" and "Progressive Local Administrations: Local Public Policy and Local-National Relations."

9. Steven R. Reed, *Japanese Prefectures and Policymaking* (Pittsburgh: University of Pittsburgh Press, 1986).

ernmental organizations (NGOs) and local internationalization, and Sheila Smith's study of former Governor Ōta and the controversial issue of U.S. military bases in Japan.

Taking the latter first, the end of the cold war has led to obvious questions, both in Japan and in the United States, about the necessity of continuing the concrete and never popular vestige of that security threat in Japan—the stationing of American military personnel on Japanese territory. Although American facilities remain in many locales in Japan, their presence is most obvious and has the most blatant impact on local residents in Okinawa, where the sheer density and scale of the bases and American military personnel intrudes in often horrendous ways on the lives of the inhabitants there. The issue of the bases reached crisis proportions in 1995 when a twelve-year-old Japanese schoolgirl was brutally raped by several American military personnel stationed on Okinawa. The incident led the incumbent governor to challenge the central governor over the issue of the bases. But as Smith points out, Ōta's crusade signified a more general issue of center-local relations than just the immediate one of U.S. facilities because he "challenged also the way in which the wishes of local communities are translated into national policy choices."

Tegtmeyer Pak's article represents an increasingly broader trend in the post-cold war social sciences—attention to the escalating level of global contacts and influence among nongovernmental organizations. Social scientists are beginning to recognize that internationalization is a question not only of increased communication among national governments and enhanced levels of trade between greater numbers of economies, but also of the increasingly active role played by private groups—both for and not for profit—in international affairs and relationships. In this case, Tegtmeyer Pak looks at the issue of foreign migrant workers in Japan—an issue that was nonexistent before the economic "bubble" of the 1980s created a labor shortage and many guest workers entered Japan both legally and a-legally. Here, NGOs in local governments have tried to face and manage an issue that the national government either has pretended did not exist or has not handled well.

The second major change in Japanese politics in the 1990s was the salience of the issue of "reform." Spurred by several cases of revealed gross corruption among politicians, and more recently among the once-vaunted and seemingly incorruptible central bureaucrats, Japan has experienced more calls for reform, and more actual, structural reform, than at any time since the Occupation. In 1994, for example, new electoral and campaign finance laws were passed that fundamentally changed the

Japanese electoral system for the House of Representatives. Administrative reform, an issue that also was popular in the 1980s and that resulted in the privatization of several of Japan's major public corporations,[10] is also being pursued into new areas. One of these reforms involves the reorganization of the Japanese bureaucracy. Another, still in process, is of center-local relations and is likely to fundamentally lessen the delegation of administrative functions to local governments, but not their dependence on the center for funds.

Patricia L. Maclachlan deals with another, and local, element of the recent calls for reform in Japan—increasing revelations of corruption and unethical practices among local bureaucrats. Comparing them to the citizens' movements of the 1960s and 1970s, she examines how local citizens groups have used public disclosure laws to reveal such practices. Her article indicates that despite the fading of local affairs and citizens' movements from attention both in the Japanese media and in American academia, the spirit of local civic action that flared so brilliantly in the 1970s may still be alive and well a quarter century later in some parts of Japan.

Ted Gilman's article presents us with a startling contrast. Here, exploring urban redevelopment politics and policy-making in Omuta, he finds that citizen input is given only nominal response and that this area of policy-making is still highly traditional and dominated by the entrenched bureaucratic experts. Reading his article in conjunction with Maclachlan's, one is struck by the disparate elements of continuity and discontinuity between the second and third waves of attention to local affairs. The obvious question is whether Gilman's findings are relatively unique to a certain type of locale, or to the particular policy arena he is dealing with, or whether they are actually much more common in local policy-making than we might have expected given the rhetoric of citizen participation at the local level since the 1970s. In short, we need to find out whether and how the changes at the local level over two decades ago were institutionalized in both politics and political consciousness, and the extent to which they were an aberration, after which it was "Same

---

10. On the causes, process, and consequences of administrative reform in the 1980s, see Michio Muramatsu and Ellis S. Krauss, "Japan: The Paradox of Success," in Johan P. Olsen and B. Guy Peters, eds., *Lessons from Experience: Experiential Learning in Administrative Reforms in Eight Democracies* (Oslo and Boston: Scandinavian University Press, 1996), 214-42; Mike Mochizuki, "Public Sector Labor and the Privatization Challenge: The Railway and Telecommunications Unions," in Gary D. Allinson and Yasunori Sone, eds., *Political Dynamics in Contemporary Japan* (Ithaca: Cornell University Press, 1993), 181-99.

old, same old," as Gilman puts it. Pat Steinhoff's concluding essay prepares the groundwork for this future research by exploring in more detail and complexity the various types of relationships between *kan* (officials) and *min* (people) found in this new wave of research. What future research can do is discover where, to what extent, and why, each type of relationship is found in Japan's local politics and policy-making.

There is one dimension of center-local relations on which all the papers below agree: there is room for far more local initiative—whether stimulated by established authorities or citizens—than the old stereotype of one-third local autonomy and a centralized bureaucratic state would suggest. In this respect at least, second- and third-wave research is in substantial agreement.

In another sense, we may hope that this "third wave" of scholarship on the local level in Japanese politics represents a discontinuity in Japanese studies in the U.S.: whereas the previous generation's attention to the subject dissipated and they moved on to new subjects along with the headlines, it is profoundly to be hoped that this wave will itself become institutionalized and lead to a continuous subfield of local politics within the field. Another good sign in that direction in addition to the work that follows is that one of the leading scholars of local politics in Japan, Muramatsu Michio, who like his American counterparts focused more on national politics for many years, has published a book on *Local Power in the Japanese State* that has recently been translated into English.[11] There are enough good scholars in Japanese politics now to support such a subfield without detracting from the quantity and quality of research on national and international issues involving Japan. In short, let us hope this current rise in the ocean represents a permanent rise in sea level and not just another passing wave.

11. Michio Muramatsu, *Local Power in the Japanese State*, trans. Betsey Scheiner and James White (Berkeley: University of California Press, 1997).

Information Disclosure and the Center-Local Relationship in Japan

Patricia L. Maclachlan

In the summer of 1995,[1] news of an intergovernmental practice dubbed *kankansettai*[2] began sweeping the headlines of local Japanese newspapers. Loosely translated as "receptions among bureaucrats," *kankansettai* connotes the efforts of prefectural officials to wrest favors from their national counterparts by wining and dining them at the taxpayers' expense. As one might expect, the evidence scattered in the wake of this practice is the stuff of which journalist dreams are made. Stories abound, for example, of bureaucratic schmoozing over bottles of wine costing tens of thousands of yen; of lavish dinners at Tokyo's finest restaurants; and of visits to hot-spring resorts with expensive geisha in tow.

As if that were not enough, disgruntled local taxpayers have also been bombarded with news of *karashutchō* (fictitious business trips),[3] a practice involving official funds earmarked for business trips that are either pocketed by officials or used for private vacations. In Hokkaido, a number of bureaucrats who were accused of *karashutchō* were members of the very committees charged with investigating the practice.[4] According to one source, financial misappropriations in twenty-two prefectures

1. I would like to thank John Campbell, Ellis Krauss, T.J. Pempel, Patricia Steinhoff, and Bartholomew Sparrow for their encouragement and valuable comments on earlier drafts of this essay. I am also grateful to Mindy Kotler, Holly Ogren, and Shinju Fujihara for their bibliographic, editorial, and substantive suggestions.
2. The term *kankansettai* was apparently coined in 1995 and quickly became one of the top ten new words of the year. "Shimin ga kyōkan, zenkoku e hakyō," *Kōbe Shimbun*, April 28, 1997.
3. David Alan Boling, "Information Disclosure in Japan: Local Governments Take the Lead," paper presented to the Fifth International Conference on Japanese Information in Science, Technology, and Commerce, U.S. Library of Congress (July 30–August 1, 1997), p. 129.
4. Moriya Toshiharu, *Chihō jichitai no jōhōkōkai to kansa* (Tokyo: Chūō Keizaisha, 1997), 221.

involving both *kankansettai* and *karashutchō* totaled over forty billion yen and implicated roughly 20,000 local officials in early 1998.[5]

Tales of governmental corruption in Japan are certainly nothing new. What is noteworthy, however, is the manner in which evidence of *kankansettai* and *karashutchō* was first uncovered. Across the country, networks of citizen groups banded together to request documentation of these practices under local and prefectural information disclosure ordinances. When the localities refused to grant those requests, the groups would either appeal the decisions to local governmental review committees or take their cases to court. By 1996, over sixty lawsuits had either been heard or were before the bench; more are still pending.

Much more than just an effort to expose corruption at the local, prefectural, and intergovernmental levels, these lawsuits represented deliberate attempts by local citizen activists to highlight both the flaws of local information disclosure rules and the need for a national disclosure law. Many of their goals have already been achieved. A number of localities, for instance, have cracked down on spending irregularities and tightened their disclosure rules. In May 1999, moreover, after two decades of citizen pressure and governmental debate, the Diet finally passed a national information disclosure law. Hailed as one of the few statutes initiated by and for average citizens in recent years,[6] the new law will significantly enhance levels of governmental transparency[7] and accountability.

In this paper, I explore information disclosure as a case study in local and prefectural policy innovation, the effects of such innovation on policy-making at the center, and the nature of state-society relations as revealed through center-local linkages. Following a brief literature review that puts the disclosure case into a comparative context, I trace the history of this issue at all levels of government and highlight the main features of local disclosure ordinances. In subsequent sections, I analyze

5. "Revised Information Acts Would Quell Expense Abuses," *Asahi Evening News*, February 24, 1998.
6. Other examples of recently enacted "citizen" laws include the 1998 Nonprofit Organization Law (NPOhō) and the 1994 Products Liability Law (PLhō). As with the Information Disclosure Law, however, both of these laws are weakened by provisions that reflect some of the demands of their opponents. For more on the products libability statute, see Patricia L. Maclachlan, "Protecting Producers from Consumer Protection: The Politics of Products Liability Reform in Japan," *Social Sciences Japan Journal* 2.2 (November 1999).
7. For more on the issue of enhanced governmental transparency in Japan, see Jean Heilman Grier, "The Need for a More Transparent and Accessible Administrative System in Japan," paper presented to the Fifth International Conference on Japanese Information in Science, Technology, and Commerce, U.S. Library of Commerce (July 30–August 1, 1997).

the political circumstances surrounding policy-making since the early 1990s and then compare the disclosure recommendations of the influential Administrative Reform Council (Gyōsei Kaikaku Iinkai) to local norms in an effort to understand the impact of local developments on national policy-making. I conclude with an overview of the new law and a discussion of the implications of its legislative history for our understanding of local policy innovation and citizen activism in Japan.

LITERATURE REVIEW

Knowledge of center-local linkages, local policy innovation, and citizen activism at the local level in Japan has expanded significantly over the past three decades. The proliferation of progressive local governments during the 1960s and 1970s spawned several important studies that have enhanced our appreciation of the potential for local autonomy and local innovation within a centralized intergovernmental system,[8] and of the opportunities at the local level for citizen groups to articulate their preferences. In a path-breaking volume edited by Steiner, Krauss, and Flanagan, for example, scholars explore political, party, or policy conflict between the central and local governments in an effort to determine the extent to which local groups can successfully oppose the policies of the center.[9] Primarily concerned with the implications of their findings for changes in the incidence and quality of citizen participation, the authors also conclude that the politicization of local politics has been "breathing new life into the local autonomy principle"[10] by encouraging local chief executives to engage in policy innovation and to articulate local citizen preferences to the center.

Richard Samuels's work on the dynamics of the policy process confronts the center-local relationship more directly and provides important insight into the patterns of local dynamism. Taking issue with the notion that government in Japan is completely structured along vertical lines,[11] Samuels identifies six categories of horizontal or "translocal" activity between local governmental actors: policy implementation, communication, budgetary acquisition, support for and opposition to cen-

---

8. Richard J. Samuels, *The Politics of Regional Policy in Japan: Localities Incorporated?* (Princeton: Princeton University Press, 1983), xxi.
9. Kurt Steiner, Ellis S. Krauss, and Scott C. Flanagan, eds., *Political Opposition and Local Politics in Japan* (Princeton: Princeton University Press, 1980), 7–8.
10. Ibid., 446.
11. Samuels, *The Politics of Regional Policy in Japan*, xxi.

tral policies, and, more rarely, policy proposition.[12] On the basis of his findings vis-à-vis regional policy, he concludes that policy initiatives emanating directly from below or from within these translocal linkages are "not inconsistent with the imperatives of centralized public administration."[13]

Steven R. Reed comes to a similar conclusion in his study of the relationship between the central government and the prefectures. "Local governments," he notes, "need not have much authority, much financial autonomy, or particularly democratic politics to be effective institutions."[14] In the environmental realm, Reed explains how some localities set strict effluent and SO_2 standards that surpassed the standards set by the Environmental Agency, yet he could find no evidence of efforts on the part of the center to revoke ordinances that exceeded the limits of national law.[15]

Muramatsu Michio's book on local power expands the boundaries of local autonomy and innovation even further. Like Steiner, Krauss, and Flanagan. Muramatsu is interested not only in relations between levels of governmental administration,[16] but also in the activities of citizen groups and politicians that are mediated alongside or through local governmental institutions. He envisions, in other words, "A relationship of overlapping authority in which central-local relations are mediated in part by politics,"[17] and that leads to a "demonstration effect" of policy initiatives not only *between* localities, but between the localities and the center as well.[18] Muramatsu goes on to hypothesize that "the extent of local influence on the state is proportionate to the extent of local politicization,"[19] a hypothesis that also holds true, albeit with some modifications, in the information disclosure case.

In keeping with Muramatsu's findings, the information disclosure case is highly politicized in that it involves vertical linkages between the localities and the center, horizontal linkages between the localities, and linkages between networks of citizen groups and local institutions. Unlike many of the cases examined by the works mentioned above, however, the disclosure case has not involved direct confrontation between

12. Ibid., 18–32.
13. Ibid., 245.
14. Steven R. Reed, *Japanese Prefectures and Policymaking* (Pittsburgh: University of Pittsburgh Press, 1986), 170.
15. Ibid., 85.
16. Michio Muramatsu, *Local Power in the Japanese State*, translated by Betsey Scheiner and James White (Berkeley: University of California Press, 1997), 5.
17. Ibid., 35.
18. Ibid., 47.
19. Ibid., 126.

local administrations and their central counterpart for control over local affairs. In the 1990s, many local governmental institutions—together with the courts—have been used primarily as neutral channels of interest articulation for individual citizens and networks of translocal citizen groups intent on bringing about behavioral change at *both* the central and local levels; local officials, for the most part, have been targets—rather than participants—of local activism. Consequently, and to rephrase Muramatsu, the extent of local influence on the state is largely proportionate to the degree of politicization not of local government, but of otherwise passive groups of local citizens.[20] As the following pages will attest, moreover, the level and impact of citizen activism in this case have been far-reaching and at times even surprising given our stereotypical images of a passive Japanese political culture.[21]

The information disclosure case is also unusual in terms of patterns or flows of policy-related influence. Whereas the environmental and most other cases of local innovation involved primarily bottom-up flows of influence, flows in the disclosure case have been multi-directional. As will be examined in greater detail later on, citizen lawsuits filed under local ordinances have had a significant impact on national policymaking, which in turn has prompted the localities to reform their own disclosure ordinances. Influence has also flowed in horizontal directions; citizen groups followed the lead of entrepreneurial citizens in a handful of localities by making active use of local grievance resolution mechanisms, while the efforts of a few local and prefectural governments to reform their disclosure rules produced a demonstration effect that quickly spread across the country.

In sum, the information disclosure case is a rare example of an interactive *process* of policy innovation and proposition involving all levels of government, citizen groups, and, in recent years, the courts. As will become increasingly apparent in subsequent pages, moreover, this process has involved the use of institutionalized channels of local grievance articulation in ways that were not intended by the ordinances that established them.

---

20. I make similar observations in my work on consumer movement activism and consumer protection policy-making. Consumer activists frequently work through local governmental institutions in their efforts to mold public opinion on particular policy proposals at the center. Patricia L. Maclachlan, "The Politics of Consumer Protection in Japan: The Impact of Consumer Organizations on Policy Making," Ph.D. diss., Columbia University, 1996.
21. Boling makes the same point with reference to citizen litigation under local disclosure ordinances in, "Information Disclosure in Japan: Local Governments Take the Lead."

THE PRE-1993 HISTORY OF INFORMATION DISCLOSURE

Information disclosure laws establish a specific relationship between private citizens and governmental officials whereby the latter are obligated to release public documents to citizens upon demand. Among the countries with such legislation in place are Austria, Australia, Canada, Denmark, France, Holland, and Sweden. Neither Germany nor England have enacted disclosure laws, although the latter is currently moving toward a more open system.[22] The American Freedom of Information Act, enacted in 1966 and amended in 1974 in the wake of the Watergate scandal, is one of the most progressive disclosure laws in the world and served as a model for advocates in Japan.

Japanese proponents upheld the individual's alleged "right to know" (*shiru kenri*) as the fundamental basis of information disclosure. In fact, many argued that the right to know is inherent in the constitutional provisions for freedom of expression; without ready access to information, or so the argument went, citizens cannot be expected to express themselves freely and effectively. Accordingly, advocates argued, the right to know should be clearly stated as the primary objective of disclosure rules. Many legal scholars, by contrast, noted that the concept is not firmly established in legal precedent, let alone stipulated in the constitution; nor, they argued, does it constitute the primary objective of foreign disclosure laws.[23] To them, the foremost objective of disclosure should be "openness" (*kōkaisei*) and governmental accountability (*setsumei sekinin*)[24] with an eye to promoting citizen participation in governmental affairs.

Efforts to enact a national disclosure law in Japan go back a long way. The issue was first debated among academics during the early 1970s in response to international trends—particularly developments within the American system. On the heels of the Lockheed scandal of the mid-1970s, disclosure became a public issue as the opposition parties, consumer organizations, the Japan Civil Liberties Union (Jiyū Jinken Kyōkai), and other citizen groups pressured policymakers for greater levels of openness and accountability.[25] It was not until the Ohira administration, however, that information disclosure was finally elevated onto the governmental agenda at the national level.

---

22. Matsui Shigenori, *Jōhōkōkaihō* (Tokyo: Iwanami Shinsho, 1996), 9.
23. See, for example, Abe Yasutaka, *Jōhōkōkai: ronsō, teian* (Tokyo: Nihon Hyoronsha, 1997), 6–8.
24. Ibid., 6.
25. Horibe Masao, "Jōhōkōkaihō yōkōan no haikei to jōhōkōkai jorei no hikaku," *Jurisuto*, 1093 (July 1, 1996): 14.

The catalyst behind this development was the formation in October 1979 of a coalition government between the Liberal Democratic Party (LDP) and the New Liberal Club (NLC), and the LDP's acquiescence to the latter's demand for high-level deliberations on disclosure. Prime Minister Ohira, who had been predisposed to enactment prior to the coalition's formation, regularly fielded questions about disclosure during the subsequent Diet session and openly pressed for movement on the issue. In early 1980, the cabinet took a small step toward openness when it resolved to encourage bureaucrats to be more forthright in offering information to the public.[26]

Bureaucratic resistance, the sudden death of Prime Minister Ohira in 1980, and the LDP's resounding victory at the polls combined to usher in a new stage of deliberations at the national level. On the surface of things, discussions seemed to be moving along at a busy pace: blue ribbon advisory commissions like the Rinji Gyōsei Chōsakai explored the issue; the Administration Management Agency established a special facility to coordinate bureaucratic deliberations (Jōhōkōkai Mondai Kenkyūkai),[27] and the opposition parties continued to raise the subject in the Diet. Without the support of the increasingly passive and conservative LDP, however, this flurry of activity amounted to little more than public posturing. For all intents and purposes, an unexpected window of opportunity in favor of enactment had closed.

The initiative consequently passed to the localities. Demands for open information were particularly strong at the local and prefectural levels in response to the legacy of a comparatively close relationship between residents and progressive localities and the burgeoning belief that information disclosure was a prerequisite for effective grass-roots participation in politics.[28] Standing at the vanguard of the pro-disclosure movement was a wide array of citizen groups: The Japan Federation of Housewives' Associations (Shufuren), the first citizens' organization to openly criticize the lack of transparency of governmental advisory commissions;[29] The Consumers' Union of Japan (Nihon Shōhisha Renmei), the first nongovernment organization to advocate the enactment of an

---

26. Hayashi Shuzo, "Jōhōkōkai seidō no genjo to kongo no kadai," *Toshi mondai kenkyū* 37.1 (January 1985): 7.
27. Akita Hidoshi, "Jichitai no jōhōkōkai seido no genjō kara manabu mono," *Jiyū to seigi* 46.5 (May 1995): 42.
28. Matsui, *Jōhōkōkaihō*, 27.
29. Mitake Jiro, "Jōhōkōkaihō to shōhisha," *Shōhisha nettowaaku* 46 (May 1995): 2. Shufuren representatives have sat on consumer-related advisory commissions at both the national and local levels since the 1960s, and since then they have been demanding that *shingikai* proceedings and documentation be more readily accessible to the public.

American-style information disclosure law;[30] the Japan Civil Liberties' Union, which had been interested in open access to information since the thalidomide scandal and other cases involving illnesses resulting from tainted medicines and food products;[31] and countless town- and city-specific organizations that had formed in direct response to the issue. Allied with the lawyers' associations, legal scholars, the media,[32] and opposition party politicians, these groups campaigned vigorously for the enactment of information disclosure ordinances at both the local and prefectural levels.

The localities responded quickly to these demands by launching formal deliberations on the topic with ample opportunity for regular citizen input. In March 1982, Japan's first information disclosure ordinance was enacted in the town of Kanayama in Yamagata Prefecture. Later that same year, Kanagawa became the first prefecture to introduce formal disclosure rules, and others quickly followed suit in what was clearly a case of intergovernmental competition. Of the first prefectures to jump on the disclosure bandwagon, most, including Kanagawa, Tokyo, Saitama, Kyoto, and Osaka, were or had recently been run by progressive governments. By the end of the decade, however, with thirty-six prefectural and 136 city and town ordinances in place, the trend had crossed party lines to embrace conservative administrations as well.[33] Those numbers continued to increase during the 1990s, reaching forty-seven prefectures and 348 cities and towns by the summer of 1997.[34] This trend seems indicative of what Gary Allinson has referred to as the "suprapartisan qualities" of conservative governments that were established following the era of progressive local administrations of the late 1960s and 1970s.[35]

INFORMATION DISCLOSURE ORDINANCES

Although the objectives of information disclosure ordinances varied from locality to locality, most had in common at least a few of the following

---

30. Ibid., 3.
31. Ibid.
32. The national print media has been an important component of the pro-disclosure movement, although not always an enthusiastic one. Conventional wisdom has it that many journalists feared disclosure on the grounds that it would encourage the "scoop," thereby contributing to the breakdown of the cloistered and exclusive reporters' clubs connected to individual ministries.
33. Hiramatsu Tsuyoshi, "Jōhōkōkai," *Jurisuto* 1000 (May 1, 1995): 49.
34. "394 jichitai de dōnyū," *Asahi Shimbun*, June 3, 1996. In 1996, Nara became the last prefecture to enact a disclosure ordinance.
35. Gary D. Allinson, *Japan's Postwar History* (Ithaca, NY: Cornell University Press, 1997), 161.

interrelated aims: the promotion of citizen participation in local government; the enhancement of citizen trust in and understanding of local administration; the promotion of the impartial implementation of government policy; and the realization of governmental openness.[36] Only three ordinances—those of Tokyo, Okinawa, and Osaka—recognized the citizen's "right to know";[37] the rest simply specified the citizen's "right to request information."

Public documents that qualified for disclosure before the new national disclosure law was enacted were normally limited to those generated by the executive branch of government; only a handful of localities also subjected their legislative assemblies to the purview of the law.[38] Like the American disclosure system, documents were considered "open" (kōkai) unless specified otherwise. Unlike the American system, however, exemptions were numerous and included:

1. information relating to police functions and public safety;
2. information that has a bearing on an individual's privacy;
3. business secrets;
4. information that could jeopardize the implementation of policy;
5. information relating to relations with other levels of government;[39]
6. information that could impede the governmental deliberative process.[40]

As citizens' groups discovered, these exemptions were often vaguely worded and subject to manipulation by officials looking for excuses to withhold information. Moreover, there were numerous cases in which local officials defined the term "public document"[41] very narrowly in order to avoid disclosure, or refused to admit that public documentation on a particular issue even existed.

The procedures for requesting information were quite similar across localities and were clearly stipulated by law. The vast majority of ordinances required those who requested information to be not only Japanese citizens, but also either residents or employees of businesses located

36. Kantō Bengoshika Rengōkai, ed., *Tsukaikonasō jōhōkōkai seido* (Tokyo: Meiseki Shoten, 1997), 70.
37. Abe, *Jōhōkōkai: ronsō, teian*, 6.
38. "Tōdōfuken: gikai, teisatsu ni mo jōhōkōkai no ugoki," *Yomiuri Shimbun*, October 20, 1997.
39. Technically, documents pertaining to the execution of entity-assigned functions are not subject to disclosure. In practice, however, some localities will release such information unless specifically instructed by the central government not to.
40. Matsui, *Jōhōkōkaihō*, 75–87.
41. "Revised Information Acts Would Quell Expense Abuse."

within the locality in question.[42] When requesting a particular document, a citizen was normally required to fill out forms at a special designated office or "information wicket" (*jōhō seikyū madoguchi*) within the local bureaucracy. Once those forms were submitted, officials within the bureau or office that produced that particular document would decide among themselves whether or not it should be subject to disclosure. If the decision was to disclose (*kōkai*), the requester would receive either photocopies of the document through the mail or a notice informing him or her to proceed to a designated governmental office where the original document could be read.

If the decision was "nondisclosure" (*hikōkai*),[43] the citizen could appeal the decision in either of two ways. First, he or she could appeal (*fufuku moshitate*) to a local governmental review committee (*fufuku kansaiin*) established to deal expressly with disclosure cases. Members of these committees were selected by the chief executive with the approval of the legislative assembly.[44] Although the recommendations of these committees were usually followed by the bureau in question, officials were free to disregard them since they did not have the force of law behind them.[45]

If citizens were dissatisfied with the governmental appeal route, or if they simply preferred to bypass that avenue altogether, they could take their case to court in the hopes of obtaining a legally binding reversal of the nondisclosure decision. These were the lawsuits that were making headlines in the mid-1990s. We turn now to an examination of the circumstances surrounding their proliferation.

INFORMATION DISCLOSURE IN THE 1990S

Since information disclosure first became an issue in Japan, bureaucrats at the national level looked upon the possibility of opening their ranks to the scrutiny of the public with nothing short of alarm. Accordingly,

---

42. Kawasaki city is the only locality in Japan to allow anyone—including foreigners—to request information under its disclosure ordinance.

43. Lawrence Repeta notes that the decisions of these committees tend to reflect the structure of their membership; those that are populated primarily by liberal academics and lawyers tend to be more pro-disclosure than those consisting of friends of the chief executive. See Repeta, "The Future of Information Disclosure in Japan," typescript, March 27, 1998, p. 6.

44. Moriya, *Chihō jichitai no jōhōkōkai to kansa*, 9.

45. Shimizu Hideo, "Jōhōkōkaihō seido o meguru konnichi no dōkō," *Jiyū to seigi* 46.5 (May 1995): 8.

measures such as the 1991 adoption of nonbinding disclosure standards by the government of the day were largely ignored by officials or followed in a perfunctory manner.[46] By the Hosokawa administration, however, the enactment of a comprehensive information disclosure law became a distinct possibility for the first time since the Ohira administration. Hosokawa and his successor, Prime Minister Hata (both of whom supported the idea of disclosure in principle), underscored the need for early enactment in speeches to the Diet, and oversaw the establishment of facilities throughout the bureaucracy to promote further discussion on the issue.

The momentum picked up even more under Prime Minister Murayama, another long-standing and enthusiastic proponent of disclosure. It was under Murayama's watch that the Administrative Reform Council was established in late 1994, complete with an Administrative Information Disclosure Committee (Gyōsei Jōhōkōkai Bukai) to deliberate exclusively on disclosure. The final report of this committee was submitted to Prime Minister Hashimoto in December 1996 and formed the basis of the freedom of information bill that was submitted to the Diet in the spring of 1998.

Throughout his administration, Murayama was well aware of bureaucratic resistance to the proposed law and encouraged citizen activists in their efforts to build up a large public constituency in favor of enactment.[47] Fired up by what appeared to be an unprecedented window of opportunity, networks of private citizens were formed or expanded around the country to pressure local governments into reforming their disclosure rules and to call for the enactment of a national law.

Citizen activism was carried out against a backdrop of legal and political developments that, when combined with the opportunities created by the LDP's temporary fall from power in 1993 and the rise of more pro-consumer progressive governments, established a political environment in favor of enactment at the national level and reform at the local level. First, information disclosure was increasingly viewed as a logical component of administrative reform that aimed to increase the transparency of governmental proceedings.[48] A significant step in this direction was achieved with the enactment of the Administrative Procedures Act (Gyōsei Tetsuzukihō) in 1994. This law differs from an information disclosure law, however, in that it only accords individuals whose inter-

---

46. Matsui, *Jōhōkōkaihō*, 195–96.
47. Shimizu, "Jōhōkōkaihō seido o meguru konnichi no dōkō," 9.
48. For more on this issue, see Grier, "The Need for a More Transparent and Accessible Administrative System in Japan."

ests are directly affected by a particular administrative act the right to view pertinent documentation.[49] Second, adequate disclosure provisions were also deemed a necessary prerequisite to the successful implementation of "self-responsibility" (jiko sekinin), the principle of deregulation that makes consumers and producers—rather than regulatory agencies of government—ultimately responsible for their own well-being. Third, the need for binding disclosure rules was further highlighted by the 1994 enactment of a strict liability law, the effectiveness of which can only be guaranteed if governmental information pertaining to dangerous products is made readily available to the public at large. Fourth, foreign pressure has also played a limited but significant role. Since 1994, the U.S. has been urging Japan to enact an information disclosure law as part of its overall demands for greater levels of administrative transparency in Japan.[50] Juxtaposed over these developments was a steady string of scandals, including the jusen (housing-loan corporations) and tainted-blood incidents, which simply highlighted the government's lack of transparency and its apparent unwillingness to disclose information in a fair and timely manner.

Citizen activism vis-à-vis information disclosure in this new political environment took a number of forms. At the individual level, residents were making regular, if not frequent, use of information disclosure ordinances to request information on issues as varied as education, public works, health, and product safety.[51] Between 1983 and 1993 in Kanagawa Prefecture, for instance, over 1,400 residents filed for disclosure.[52] The fact that the ordinances were being used did not mean that citizens were satisfied with them; on the contrary, many complained of slipshod procedures, rude officials, lengthy delays, and bureaucratic denials of formal requests on vague or legally dubious grounds.[53] Ironically, local governmental procedures to guarantee transparency had created public expectations that the procedures themselves ultimately proved incapable of fulfilling.

Accordingly, many citizen groups organized or expanded translocal networks that coordinated efforts to highlight flaws in the system. In September 1995, for example, consumer groups in thirty localities around the country applied to their pertinent disclosure authori-

---

49. Fujiwara Shizuo, "Jōhōkōkai jorei to gyōsei tetsuzukihō," *Toshi mondai* 85.10 (October 1994): 68.
50. Shimizu, "Jōhōkōkai seidō o meguru konnichi no dōkō," 5.
51. Repeta, "The Future of Information Disclosure in Japan," 7–8.
52. Shimizu, "Jōhōkōkai seido o meguru konnichi no dōkō," 8.
53. Interview, Hiwasa Nobuko (President, Shōdanren), December 18, 1997.

ties for the names of both the brands and manufacturers of hazardous household appliances. Only three of the thirty localities, however, released the requested information. In addition, many of the officials manning the information wickets were unfamiliar with the disclosure procedures or were difficult to deal with, and several localities took weeks to complete the necessary paperwork.[54] The experiment underscored both the absence of uniform disclosure standards across the localities and the lack of transparency of local consumer bureaucracies. It also helped galvanize the expansion of the consumer-led Citizen's Network for the Establishment of an Information Disclosure Law (Jōhōkōkaihō no Settei o Motomeru Shimin Nettowaaku), a network of national and local consumer organizations, environmental and human rights groups, legal scholars, and lawyers that had been established in 1980.

In a similar vein, the National Liaison Council of Citizen Ombudsmen (Zenkoku Shimin Ombuzuman Renrakukai), a national, nongovernmental network of lawyers and private citizens formed in 1994 around the disclosure issue,[55] worked to expose both the misappropriation of public funds and the lack of transparency at the prefectural and local levels. For example, it managed to uncover evidence under information disclosure ordinances of ¥5.3 billion in food, drink, and other entertainment expenditures within forty prefectural governments for fiscal year 1993 alone. Much of that money, it is believed, was used to influence officials at the national level.[56]

In 1996, the liaison council conducted a well-publicized experiment to determine the degree of transparency of local disclosure systems and to uncover the extent of *kankansettai* and *karashutchō* at the prefectural level. On a specified day in October, the council submitted disclosure applications to all forty-seven prefectures for information on the entertainment and travel expenses of local officials. Based on the responses, it ranked the prefectures according to levels of openness and compiled a group "report card"[57] in which the average prefectural score (out of 100) stood at a mere 42 points.[58] The reasons cited for the dismal

---

54. Nishijima Hideko, "Jōhōkōkai jōrei de shōhin no anzensei o chekku!" *Shōhisha nettowaaku* 50 (January 1996): 21–27.
55. Sugiura Hideki, "Shimin ombuzuman no mezasu mono to seido no arikata," *Shōhisha nettowaaku* 52 (November 1996): 15–16.
56. Matsui, *Jōhōkōkaihō*, 153.
57. "Jōhōkōkai: rakudai tōken ari," *Asahi Shimbun*, February 4, 1997.
58. Ibid. Miyagi Prefecture ranked the highest out of the forty-seven prefectures in terms of openness, Okinawa second, Osaka sixteenth, Kyoto twenty-eighth, Tokyo thirty-third, and Yamagata Prefecture last.

showings included the use of vague or legally dubious excuses to back up decisions of nondisclosure (for example, many localities refused to release the names of officials who were spending public money for private purposes on the grounds that it would violate their right to privacy), lengthy administrative delays lasting up to two to three months, the mysterious disappearance of documents that were known to exist, and high user and photocopying fees.[59] The report card, which was extensively covered by all the major dailies, reinforced public suspicions that the localities had something to hide and heightened awareness of the lack of administrative transparency at the prefectural level.

Several groups within the liaison council immediately appealed the decisions through the courts. Many of these cases, as well as the sixty or so other *kankansettai* and *karashutchō* cases that had been filed independently of the liaison committee's experiment, have been decided in favor of the plaintiffs, much to the chagrin of local authorities who must now release information about bureaucratic spending habits that they would just as soon keep under wraps. In other instances, the negative publicity surrounding the results of the liaison committee's experiment was all it took to prompt prefectural governors to reverse their original decisions and release the controversial information. Some cases even went as far as the Supreme Court. Much more conservative than their local counterparts, however, the Supreme Court tended to rule in favor of local bureaucrats.[60] All in all, these cases have revealed an unprecedented level of activism at the district court level—not to mention a willingness on the part of local citizens to use litigation as an instrument of political expression.[61]

The public's intolerance of the lack of bureaucratic openness surrounding the alleged misappropriation of public funds also forced local governmental review committees to work overtime. According to a survey conducted by the *Nikkei Shimbun*, there were 178 disclosure-related appeals heard by committees across the country in 1996 alone, 36 of them in Tokyo.[62]

The effects of all this activity on governmental propriety, prospects for enhanced governmental transparency, and intergovernmental relations have been significant. The Ministry of Home Affairs, for instance, recently issued a directive to localities urging them to conduct

59. "Rakudai Jichitai Imada ni Oku..." *Asahi Shimbun*, February 4, 1997.
60. Boling, "Information Disclosure in Japan," 128.
61. Ibid.
62. "Jūmin kansaseikyū ga zōka," *Nihon Keizai Shimbun*, February 18, 1997.

their expenditures in a manner that would "avoid public criticism."[63] One locality after another, moreover, has announced the abolition of *kankansettai* and *karashutchō* and has pledged to both reduce and monitor the food, drink, and other entertainment expenses of local officials. More significantly, many localities have agreed to make all official documentation relating to such expenditures completely open to the public. Meanwhile, there is mounting evidence that promises from on high are being carried out in practice. In the 1997 survey of the disclosure systems of local governments conducted by the National Liaison Council of Citizen Ombudsmen, the average rating rose to 56 out of 100 from the previous year's low of 42, while the number of prefectural governments releasing records of food- and entertainment-related expenses increased over sevenfold.[64]

Encouraged by these and other related developments, local citizen groups continue to form across the country in an effort to maintain the momentum toward reform. In 1997 the *Tōkyō Shimbun* reported on the formation of the Tokyo Network of Citizen Ombudsmen (Tōkyō Shimin Ombuzuman Nettowaaku), which is composed of groups of lawyers and private citizens working at the grass-roots level to reform the disclosure systems of the ward governments. Like its national counterpart, the primary objectives of the Tokyo network have been to serve as a translocal—or interward—system of information dissemination and to monitor the degree of transparency of ward governments.[65]

DISCLOSURE PROPOSALS AT THE NATIONAL LEVEL

The intellectual basis of the national information disclosure law that was enacted in May 1999 was the final report of the Information Disclosure Committee of the Administrative Reform Council. Released in December 1996, the recommendations of the report responded to many of the demands of citizen groups as expressed through both the localities and the courts. In many respects, moreover, they were even more progressive than the stipulations of the local ordinances. Among the features of the report that differed significantly from those of local ordinances was the recommendation that anyone—including foreigners—be permitted to apply for disclosure. (As mentioned earlier, the vast majority of local ordinances limited qualified applicants to residents of the locality.) The

63. Matsui, *Jōhōkōkaihō*, 153.
64. "Revised Information Acts Would Quell Expense Abuse."
65. "Shimin reburu de gyōsei kanshi o," *Tōkyō Shimbun*, October 11, 1997.

report also recommended that electronic information, maps and blue-prints, information contained on floppy disks, cassette tapes, and videos be subject to disclosure. Most local ordinances only targeted written docu-mentation. Third, the report parted company from local ordinances by subjecting police documentation to disclosure. Fourth, in direct response to the rulings of the courts in local *kankansettai* and *karashutchō* cases, the report recommended that the names of officials at the rank of sec-tion chief and above be open to the public.[66] This is in marked contrast to local ordinances, none of which provided for the release of the names of officials who were suspected of misappropriating public funds. Finally, categories of information that were designated closed[67] were more clearly specified in the national report than in local ordinances. Citizen groups criticized the Information Disclosure Committee report for failing to in-clude documentation generated by governmental corporations, or spe-cial juridical persons (*tokushū hōjin*), under the purview of the law, and for neglecting to even mention the citizen's "right to know." In recogni-tion of its surprisingly progressive nature, however, most gave the report a passing grade.[68]

The report of the Information Disclosure Committee not only guided the legislative process at the national level; it influenced efforts to reform ordinances at the prefectural and local levels as well. No sooner had the report been released than the Tokyo Metropolitan Government set up a committee to deliberate on the reform of its own information disclosure ordinance, a development that had a copycat effect on other localities.[69] And in what appears to be a reflection of both intracity com-petition and an effort to bring local standards in line with anticipated standards at the national level, the rate of introduction of ordinances at the town and city level accelerated. According to a recent *Yomiuri Shimbun* poll, one quarter of town and city governments had ordinances in place as of May 1, 1999, up 61% over the previous year.[70] Some of those

66. "Kondan sanka shamei, 27 tōken kaiji," *Nihon Keizai Shimbun*, November 10, 1997.
67. The committee recommended that six categories of information should in principle be closed: business secrets; information relating to public safety; information that would constitute an invasion of privacy; information pertaining to national defense; informa-tion relating to foreign relations; and information that may impinge on the "frankness" of bureaucratic discussions. Business pressure is considered the driving force behind the closure of business-related information, although the business community as a whole has officially approved of the need for a national disclosure law. Shiin Takeo, "Jōhōkōkai ni sekkyokuteki igi," *Yomiuri Shimbun*, January 29, 1997.
68. "Jōhōkōkai hōan: zentō wa tanan," *Nihon Keizai Shimbun*, January 30, 1997.
69. "Maemuki kaisei: yōmei shingi," *Yomiuri Shimbun*, November 5, 1997.
70. "Jōhōkōkaihō: Shikuchōson 1/4 ga settei," *Yomiuri Shimbun*, June 16, 1999.

new ordinances and reforms have actually outpaced national trends in that they clearly stipulate the "right to know" and include documents generated by legislative assemblies under the purview of the law. In terms of the subjection of the police to disclosure rules, however, the localities are struggling to catch up with national norms.[71] Clearly, heightened expectations for information disclosure that arose at the local level not only influenced policy-making at the center; they came full circle in a reform movement that may further transform the relationship between citizens and local and prefectural governments. That reform movement is expected to continue for several years to come.

JAPAN'S NEW INFORMATION DISCLOSURE LAW

On March 27, 1998, the Bill Regarding Disclosure of Information Held by Administrative Organizations was approved by the Hashimoto Cabinet and submitted to the Diet.[72] For a while, the future of the bill was highly uncertain given ongoing instability within the party system and a crowded legislative schedule.[73] There was also evidence of a protracted political tug-of-war between bureaucratic nay-sayers and progressive proponents of the law. Although bureaucratic resistance to disclosure had diminished significantly since the LDP's temporary fall from power in 1993,[74] signs of hostility nevertheless lingered in MITI, the Ministry of Education, and a few other ministries that had long been lukewarm toward the idea of disclosure.[75] As a result of such bureaucratic foot-dragging, clauses were inserted into the bill that exempted certain kinds of information from disclosure, removed governmental corporations from the purview of the law, and required citizens to file lawsuits with the Tokyo District Court rather than the more accessible local court system.[76]

---

71. "Jōhōkōkai jōrei: shibu, seitei isogu," *Asahi Shimbun*, November 5, 1997.
72. "Cabinet Sends Info Disclosure Bill to Diet," *Japan Times*, March 27, 1998. The bill was drafted by the Management and Coordination Agency.
73. In the spring of 1998, for example, defense-related bills and the country's ongoing economic woes prevented the disclosure bill from getting top billing in the Diet.
74. "Jōhōkōkai de teian sodate shimin to gyōsei, taiwagata ni," *Asahi Shimbun*, February 17, 1997.
75. See, for example, Habu Teruoki, "Jikkōsei no aru jōhōkōkaihō no settei o motomeru," *Jurisuto* 1093 (July 1, 1996): 46. The Economic Planning Agency appears to be the most enthusiastic bureaucratic supporter of disclosure.
76. "Cabinet Sends Info Disclosure Bill to Diet." Following the recommendations of the 1995 Administrative Reform Council Report, the bill also exempts the government from disclosing information that infringes on individual privacy, national security and Japanese diplomatic relations, business secrets, and public safety.

Some of these exemptions were comparable to those of even the most progressive foreign disclosure laws; others, however, were simply loopholes designed to protect bureaucrats from potentially embarrassing public scrutiny.

As we have seen, most of the major legwork on information disclosure was hammered out by the Hosokawa, Hata, and Murayama coalition governments. In an interesting turn of events, it appears that progress on this issue during the mid-1990s raised public expectations on disclosure that in turn compelled both the Hashimoto and Obuchi administrations to compromise. In response to citizen complaints and to the submission of rival bills to the Diet by several opposition parties in April 1998,[77] for example, Prime Minister Hashimoto agreed to insert a clause into the bill requiring the introduction of a separate disclosure bill covering governmental corporations within the next two years.[78] During Diet deliberations, moreover, the Obuchi government acquiesced to Lower House demands that citizens be permitted to file lawsuits not only with the Tokyo High Court, but also with high courts in Sapporo, Sendai, Nagoya, Osaka, Hiroshima, Takamatsu, and Fukuoka. In response to pressure from the opposition parties and the citizens of Okinawa, this provision is to be reviewed in 2003 to provide for the possible inclusion of the Naha District Court.[79]

On May 7, 1999, the bill was finally enacted in accordance with most of the recommendations of the final report of the Information Disclosure Committee. As is wont to happen with any law that is the product of protracted negotiations and compromise, Japan's new information disclosure law has been subjected to significant criticism. First, the opposition parties and citizen groups, for example, have expressed unhappiness at the fact that the law makes no mention of a citizen's "right to know." Second, the exclusion of governmental corporations from the purview of the law has also been the target of criticism; the government's promise to review this feature of the law in two years, meanwhile, has done little to appease skeptical politicians in the opposition parties who had worked hard to have this provision inserted into the law.[80] Third, Okinawans continue to complain about the inconvenience of having to

---

77. "Semigovernmental Firms to Stay in the Shadows . . . For Now," *Japan Times*, April 28, 1998. Two rival bills were submitted, one by the Japan Communist Party, and the other by a coalition consisting of the Minshutō and the Peace Reform and Liberal parties.

78. Ibid.

79. "Upper House Clears Porn, Info Bills," *Japan Times*, April 28, 1999.

80. Interview, Haraguchi Kazuhiro, Democratic Party Lower House Dietmember, July 1, 1999.

travel to Fukuoka in order to file suit under the law's provisions, a feature of the law they find nothing short of discriminatory. Fourth, critics argue that the exact scope of nondisclosure has been kept deliberately vague in order to give bureaucrats enough discretion to keep potentially embarrassing information away from the public eye. Finally, many have complained that the national appeals board to be established under the purview of the prime minister's office will be weak and ineffective because it lacks the power to force bureaucratic compliance.[81]

The validity of these arguments notwithstanding, the new law has met with a generally favorable response from citizen activists.[82] Activists do not, however, intend to disband now that the law has been enacted. Many of the local groups and national consumer organizations that were involved in the movement to enact a freedom of information law will keep a close watch over its implementation once it finally goes into effect in 2001. To that end, they remain organized and are devising strategies to encourage citizens to activate the new statute both to test its effectiveness and to exact even more information from the government about bureaucratic practices and political corruption.

CONCLUSION

The information disclosure case is replete with political symbolism on several interrelated levels. First, the case may be indicative of a changing political culture in Japan. Just as the citizen movements of the 1960s and 1970s were hailed by analysts in the past as a realization of the ideals of political participation as stipulated by both the constitution and the Local Autonomy Law,[83] the proliferation of disclosure-related complaints and lawsuits over the past four or five years can be viewed as a product of heightened levels of political efficacy—not to mention lower tolerance levels for the corrupt practices that have long colored Japanese politics. While the disclosure case is an unusual example of citizen activism in an era of decreasing voter turnout rates and mounting political apathy, legislative developments in this issue area should nevertheless be considered alongside Japan's recently enacted Product Liability Law, the

---

81. "First Breach in the Government Wall," *Japan Times*, May 11, 1999.
82. Interviews: Shimizu Hatoko, Japan Federation of Housewives' Associations, July 8, 1999; and Hara Sanae, Consumption Science Federation, July 9, 1999.
83. Scott C. Flanagan, Kurt Steiner, and Ellis S. Krauss, "The Partisan Politicization of Local Government: Causes and Consequences," in Steiner, Krauss, and Flanagan, *Political Opposition and Local Politics in Japan*, 448.

Administrative Procedures Act, the revised Civil Lawsuits Act (Minji Soshōhō), and the recently enacted Nonprofit Organization Law, as both victories for democratic citizen groups and evidence of a small but significant increase in levels of state, prefectural, and local governmental accountability to the citizenry.

The information disclosure case also suggests a qualitative change in the priorities of grass-roots citizen groups. During the heyday of the environmental movement, citizen activists were primarily concerned about the impact of economic growth on their own well-being and that of their families. The scope of their concerns, in other words, was "local" in a psychological as well as geographic sense. The movement to improve the nation's disclosure standards, however, involves grass-roots groups consisting often of young, well-educated Japanese who have been mobilized on the basis of political principle rather than economic necessity. It is, in other words, a movement about individual rights, governmental accountability, and a host of other abstract political principles that we often associate with "good governance" in democratic polities. Veteran consumer leaders view this phenomenon as the harbinger of a new and more sophisticated wave of grass-roots democratic politics in Japan.[84] It is, quite simply, a topic worthy of further investigation.

This should not suggest, however, that citizen groups have been single-handedly responsible for progress on the disclosure issue at the national level. On the contrary, progress would have been next to impossible had it not been for shifts in political alignments at the national level and the concomitant appearance of opportunities for citizen groups to enhance their leverage over the policy-making system. In the absence of such key leaders as Ohira, Hosokawa, Hata, Murayama, and even Hashimoto—all of whom, to varying degrees, supported the notion of disclosure while residing over periods of relative LDP decline—the voices of citizen groups would not have held such sway over national policy-making.

Mention, too, must also be made of the impact of coalition governments on developments in this area. As noted earlier, most of the key deliberations taken on behalf of disclosure were initiated by coalition governments since the summer of 1993. These in turn created heightened expectations about individual rights, bureaucratic transparency, and governmental accountability—the basic democratic principles on which disclosure is based. Those coalition governments may be long gone, but it appears that both citizen groups and the opposition parties have

84. Interview, Shimizu Hatoko.

held the past two LDP governments to honoring these principles. At the risk of overgeneralizing, this may be evidence of a wave of "suprapartisan" politics at the national level comparable to what the localities have been experiencing since the 1980s.

The disclosure case also raises questions about the future of local autonomy in Japan. The issue of autonomy is not directly pertinent to this case given the lack of a legally specified authority relationship between levels of government in matters involving disclosure; the localities have complete jurisdiction over disclosure in matters controlled exclusively by local governments, and the national government has never contested this state of affairs. That said, the effects of this case may have an impact on local autonomy in the future. In light of the heightened sense of political efficacy among citizen groups that resulted from their experiences in the disclosure case, it is possible that citizen activism will eventually be channeled toward decentralization and other policies designed to strengthen the power of the localities—providing, of course, that the political opportunities are right.

Finally, and more importantly for our purposes, the disclosure case has a number of implications for our understanding of local policy innovation in the context of center-local relations and citizen activism as mediated through the localities. First, as evidenced by the recent wave of reforms to information disclosure ordinances currently under way at the prefectural and local levels, it is clear that the effects of policy innovation and promotion can flow in multiple directions at once: developments in one locality spark comparable and competitive responses in other localities; overall trends in the localities shape the terms of policy at the national level when political and economic conditions are right; and subsequent developments at the national level can loop back to the localities, prompting yet another round of innovation and reform. These findings suggest that intergovernmental relations in policy areas that have not been clearly delineated by national law can be interdependent, dynamic, and unpredictable.

When all is said and done, Japan's strong bureaucratic tradition will no doubt prevent a dramatic transformation of the relationship between Japanese citizens and their government: as noted earlier, loopholes were inserted into the new disclosure law that will enable officials to manipulate disclosure rules to their advantage; many bureaucrats will continue to treat citizens with disdain; and, in keeping with custom, much of the business of the state will be conducted behind closed doors. Any progress toward the democratization of participation in the affairs of government, in other words, is likely to be small. That said, there is ample reason to view developments in the disclosure realm with some optimism. After all, Japan's new information disclosure law grants citizens the right to at least request information from their government; if that information is refused, those citizens will be guaranteed the right to seek redress through the court system. By entrenching these rights in legislative stone, moreover, Japanese citizens have new incentives to make further demands on their governments in the future. And that can only be good for democracy.

Same Old, Same Old? Center-Local Relations in Urban Redevelopment

Theodore J. Gilman

The city of Omuta, in Fukuoka Prefecture, has a history of activism and violence in the postwar period matched by few Japanese cities its size. From 1953 through 1960, labor-management conflict at Mitsui's Miike Coal Mine in Omuta made the city a tense site of frequent and protracted strike activity. The death of one picketer drew national attention and brought the national government in Tokyo into the fray. A ten-month conflict over the downsizing of the mine workforce came to a head in the summer of 1960 when 20,000 unionists faced off with 10,000 police in full riot gear over a lockout at the mine. Nearby, 100,000 Miike union supporters from all over Japan gathered in a huge rally. Prime Minister Ikeda Hayato called on the Central Labor Relations Board (CLRB) to mediate the conflict, and the CLRB ultimately defused the situation. The board ruled that Mitsui could lay off 1,200 miners. Having agreed to accept the CLRB decision, the miners' union had no recourse. The residents of Omuta bore the brunt—and became a symbol—of the central government's decision to support big business over labor.

The city thus began a long slide into economic despair, during which it relied heavily on central government resources and handouts for support. Part one of this paper briefly illustrates Omuta's economic decline from its peak as a center of coal mining and industry. Part two records the demands and opinions of Omuta's residents as they struggled with the post-coal reality. The third part of the paper describes local government efforts to spark revitalization. Part four explains the relationship between what the people wanted and what the government actually did.

Local officials demonstrated a fair amount of autonomy vis-à-vis the central government. They decided what projects the city would do with little pressure—and considerable financial assistance—from the center. However, they also exercised a fair amount of autonomy vis-à-vis

Omuta's residents, on whose behalf they worked. City hall bureaucrats solicited public opinion regarding Omuta's post-coal future, but nonspecialists played a limited role in the city's revitalization efforts. Technocratic policy-making was the dominant mode in Omuta's redevelopment effort.

OMUTA: HISTORY AND DEMOGRAPHIC CHANGE

Omuta is the antithesis of the Japanese economic miracle. It is a Japanese city battling the effects of macroeconomic restructuring. A port city on the Ariake Sea in southern Fukuoka Prefecture on the island of Kyushu, Omuta experienced a 100-year heyday as the largest coal mining center in Japan, and during that time produced much of the energy that drove Japan's rapid 20th-century industrial growth. The Mitsui Miike mine was the largest coal mine in Japan and was the center of an extensive industrial complex that included metal smelting and processing, chemical production from coal, electricity generation, and coal mining for industrial use throughout the country. But as Japan's ability to compete with other coal-producing nations declined, demand for Miike coal declined too.

Omuta is a victim of a postwar economic double whammy: international price competition plus a global switch from coal to petroleum energy sources. As domestically produced coal either became more expensive or held its production price per ton constant, the price per ton of imported coal fell dramatically.[1] For Japanese coal consumers—mainly heavy industry and electric power producers—it made little sense to purchase domestic coal. As a result, the domestic coal-mining industry entered a period of rationalization— encouraged and supported by the Ministry of International Trade and Industry (MITI).

As Miike went, so went the community. The mine and other Mitsui production facilities provided almost 29,000 jobs for Omuta area residents in 1960. By 1991 that number had dropped to around 4,500. The impact of such a steep drop in the job base was catastrophic from the city's point of view. In addition to the steep drop in the number of jobs, the composition of jobs in Omuta changed as well. In the 1960s the ma-

1. By 1987, top-grade bituminous coal from the Miike mine was selling for ¥23,000/ton, versus ¥7,300/ton for imported coal. This was primarily due to the fact that extraction costs overseas were so much lower than in Japan. But the rise in the strength of the yen vis-à-vis the dollar also hurt the competitiveness of domestic coal. Source: Fukuoka-ken, *Fukuoka-ken santan chiiki nogenjō* (Conditions in Coal-Producing Regions of Fukuoka Prefecture) (Fukuoka, 1992), 5.

jority of jobs were in secondary, or manufacturing, industries. This was largely due to Mitsui's presence in the city. But as coal rationalization took hold and the coal-based economy started to decline, tertiary industry jobs came to outnumber manufacturing, even as the total number of employment opportunities declined over time.[2]

In Japan, when jobs dry up in a city, young people move elsewhere to find work to support their families; this certainly happened in Omuta. The population declined from a high of almost 209,000 in 1959 to slightly over 150,000 as of the 1990 national census. The largest drop occurred between 1960 and 1970, when the city lost 34,000 residents. There was a steady, though more gradual, decline from 175,000 residents in 1970 to 150,000 in 1990.

As residents moved out of the city and the population declined, the composition of the remaining population changed. The population of Omuta is increasingly made up of older citizens with no children. And as the current population continues to age, with no influx of new, younger working families to offset the trend, the number of people per family drops at about the same rate at which the population ages. This trend has not changed substantially since the major job cuts at Mitsui in the late 1960s, and the lack of change in the trend indicates two things. First, the population is getting steadily older. In 1965, 10% of the population was age 65 years or older. By 1990, that number had increased to 18%. These numbers are well above the national averages: In 1965, 6.3% of the Japanese population was age 65 years or older, while by 1990 that number had increased to 12.1%.[3]

OMUTA'S RESIDENTS VOICE THEIR WISHES FOR THE FUTURE

Following the long decline from its industrial heyday, Omuta residents began to realize that future economic security would depend on a more diversified industrial base. But how was a city with such a one-dimensional economic history supposed to create a new future for itself? Omuta residents in several sectors began initiatives they hoped would lead to positive socioeconomic changes. First, in 1986 Omuta's residents elected the first mayor in the postwar era that did not come from the Mitsui group. He had a clear mandate to develop the local economy in a new direction. Second, the city hired the Kyushu Economic Research Institute (Kyūshū

---

2. Source: National Census Data for Omuta.
3. Sōrifu Shakai Hoshō Seido Shingikai Jimukyoku, ed., *Shakai hoshō tōkei nenpō* (Social Security Statistical Yearbook) (Tokyo: Hōken, 1993), 91.

Keizai Chōsa Kyōkai, or Kyūkeichō), a nonprofit think tank, to survey public opinion on revitalizing Omuta. Finally, several community-interest groups crystallized to propose plans and get the redevelopment ball rolling.

Omuta residents showed a clear preference for moving the local economy away from coal in the mid-1980s. They also had some ideas about what local government should do to make the city more appealing. Though the citizens' wishes were achieved in the election of a mayor with a new vision for the city, that vision did not incorporate many of the policy ideas or recommendations expressed by Omuta residents.

Why did Omuta residents take decades to express these views and mobilize these post-coal ideas? The most important explanation rests in changes in national government policy. For the better part of the 1970s, Omuta's revitalization policy consisted primarily of efforts to extract compensation payments for workers who were laid off or retired early. This support money came from the continuation of the Coal Area Assistance and Promotion Policy, a national government program aimed at long-term rationalization of Omuta's main industry. The Coal Area Assistance and Promotion Policy was a long-running program administered by MITI to stabilize areas and communities hurt by the decline of the domestic coal industry. It was the earliest governmental attempt to control and soften the decline of Omuta and similar cities.

There are six laws related to coal industry decline upon which coal area policy was based. The oldest, aimed at cleaning up pollution in coal regions, was passed in 1952. The most recent, which uses tax revenue from petroleum sales to help regions cope with labor, pollution, and new industry issues, was passed in 1967. One will expire in the year 2001, while the rest are slated to expire in 2002.[4] Under these laws, a series of coal policies (*sekitan taisaku*) was promulgated by the national government for use in localities throughout Japan. The first coal policy took effect in 1963 and ran for two years. Policies two and three also had two-year durations. Subsequent policies—including the final coal policy, the ninth, which took effect in 1991[5]—had longer durations since regions became more stable and less frequent adjustments were required.

4. "Sekitan kankei roppō no gaiyō" (Summary of the Six Laws Relating to Coal), internal document received from Fukuoka Prefecture's Regional Development Division, Coal Mining Area Development Section.

5. The last program was functionally the ninth coal policy, but it was not called that because it was intended to be the final iteration in the series. According to one Fukuoka Prefecture official, simply calling it the ninth coal policy would imply an intention to make a tenth, eleventh, and so on. This was the government's way of communicating the termination of this industry rationalization policy series. Interview with Satō Seiji, Coal Mining Area Development Section Chief, Regional Development Division, Fukuoka Prefecture, May 27, 1993.

The 1984 Public Opinion Survey

In 1984 the city of Omuta commissioned Kyūkeichō to survey residents about life in Omuta. This survey, paid for by the city, was intended to lay the groundwork for a new five-year community master plan that would guide Omuta's development for the mid-1990s.[6] When the 1986 election caused a change in mayors, the results of the 1984 survey were shelved by the new administration. By the time the new mayor, Shiotsuka Kōichi, wanted to solicit resident input, almost four years had passed. City officials decided to commission a new survey in 1990 because they feared the 1984 results might be out of date.

Both public opinion surveys pointed community leaders in a fairly clear direction for change. Respondents wanted economic diversification away from the city's heavy reliance on Mitsui group enterprises. New public facilities and more appealing jobs were high on their agenda. However, the city's long history of pollution problems prompted calls for a cleaner environment and a more pleasant, green quality of life in Omuta.

Much of the 1984 survey focused on residents' attitudes toward their city. In 1984, 63% responded that Omuta was either a very easy or somewhat easy place to live (*sumi-yasui*), while 31% said it was either a moderately difficult or difficult place to live (*sumi-nikui*). When compared to neighboring cities like Kurume and Fukuoka, Omuta residents were less enthusiastic about their community. Residents of those cities rated their cities as easy places to live with greater frequency, 86% and 92%, respectively.

Citizens were divided on the elements Omuta lacked. Respondents were asked what intangible and concrete (literally) items Omuta needed most urgently. When asked to choose two (out of nine) community attitudes that city residents lacked, respondents' top three choices were "citizen unity" (29%), "local patriotism" (28%), and "helpful spirit" toward their fellow residents (26%).

On a more tangible level, respondents were asked to circle the two (out of twenty) most urgent needs for facilities facing Omuta. More parking was the number one answer in 1984 (38%). Improved higher-education facilities placed second (35%). Though there is a junior college and a

6. Kyushu Economic Research Institute, "Omuta shimin ishiki chōsa" (Omuta Residents Attitude Survey) (Fukuoka: Kyushu Economic Research Institute, 1985); Kyushu Economic Research Institute, "Omuta-shi shimin ishiki chōsa hōkokusho" (Report on the Omuta Residents Attitude Survey) (Fukuoka: Kyushu Economic Research Institute, 1990). The first survey elicited a 57.5% response rate (1,437 out of 2,500 questionnaires were returned), while the second survey received a 54.6% response rate (1,114 out of 2,040 questionnaires were returned).

technical institute in Omuta, residents must go out of town for a bachelor's degree or higher. Respondents listed sewers as the third most pressing need. More park space and more advanced medical-care facilities rounded out the top five in the 1984 survey.

Forty-two percent of respondents to the 1984 survey said the biggest physical obstacle to downtown development was the fact that the city was cut in two by the large rail complex running through the center of Omuta.[7] When asked what they thought of a proposal to elevate the rail lines and allow greater road transportation access in the downtown area, 74% said such change was either imperative or desirable. Another 17% said they did not know enough about the plan to comment on it.[8]

In 1984 Omuta residents also stated some clear tactical preferences regarding the city's overall economic redevelopment strategy. With respect to the Mitsui group, 52% thought the city should work to entice firms to move to Omuta that were not connected to Mitsui. This was a clear vote for diversification. Twenty-four percent of respondents said the city should work to use Mitsui's idle land more efficiently. Mitsui owned the vast majority of Omuta's waterfront property, and it held nearly one-third of the land within the city limits. As plants and facilities were closed, more land sat idle. Mitsui was unwilling to sell or give the land to the city.

Also in the 1984 survey, 59% said the most desirable economic development strategy was attracting new firms from outside the city. Developing existing industries came in a distant second with 14%, while promoting service sector businesses came in third with 11%. This opinion supported the widely held (71%) notion that the reason living in Omuta is difficult is that there are few appealing jobs to be found. Residents also felt that there was little activity in the city (69%) and that the city had a bad natural environment (48%).

An Economic Development Mayor

The most decisive example of public opinion in favor of a new course for Omuta came in the mayoral election of 1986. Voters elected an experienced technocrat as mayor that year. Shiotsuka Kōichi was an Omuta native who graduated from Tokyo University and worked in the national Ministry of Construction until he was elected mayor at age 36. During

7. Kyushu Economic Research Institute, 1985, 24-25.
8. The three possible responses were "imperative," "desirable," or "do not know enough to comment."

his tenure at the Construction Ministry, he spent two years on loan to the United Nations' Development Agency, working on development issues in Manila, in the Philippines. He was supported in his election bid by a right-of-center coalition (the Liberal Club, comprised of the Liberal Democratic Party, Komeitō Party, and Democratic Socialist Party) that also controlled the city assembly.

It is unclear if Shiotsuka's Construction Ministry ties helped him financially to win the election, but his experience there certainly sat well with the voters. On the surface such ties would suggest a great opportunity for Shiotsuka. However, Omuta's Lower House representative in Tokyo (Koga Makoto, LDP, six-term election winner) was chair of the Lower House Construction Committee, and this may have made it more difficult for Shiotsuka to get central government funds. The strong sense of local rivalry precluded a political alliance between Shiotsuka and Koga, and Shiotsuka ultimately challenged Koga for his Diet seat in the 1996 election; Koga rebuffed the challenge.

By far Omuta's youngest mayor ever, Shiotsuka represented a vision of a new Omuta that sought to change the city from a coal town to a more economically diversified community.[9] He brought about great changes in Omuta's revitalization efforts. Before Shiotsuka there were none; after his election, redevelopment became the city government's primary focus. The new mayor was clearly a catalyst for this change.

The 1988 Public Opinion Survey

Though the 1984 survey results seemed to suggest a strong mandate for economic development, an opinion poll published in 1988 sent a conflicting message. Table 1 lists these responses. When asked in an open-ended question what words residents wanted associated with Omuta's image in the future, environmental concerns outranked development issues by a three-to-one margin. A second open-ended question about priorities for Omuta's community building (*machi zukuri*) elicited twice as many calls for "pleasant space" (33%) as calls for "regional economic activity" (17%).[10] Omuta residents apparently were divided on the priorities for the city's future.

This underlying conflict may be explained by the fact that the 1984 survey, created and administered by Kyūkechō, an outside research

9. The city slogan, *Sekitan mo aru toshi* (The City That Has Coal Too) symbolizes this goal. This slogan received wide play in the local newspapers.
10. Omuta City, "Yutakasa afureru machi zukuri" (Community-Building with Overflowing Abundance), 1988, 26–27.

agency, offered closed-ended development-oriented choices to the respondents. When given a chance by city officials to express their own views, residents expressed quite different preferences.

Table 1. Omuta Public Attitudes Survey, 1988

Words you want associated with Omuta's future image:

1. Green	65%
2. Clean air	61%
3. Easy living	58%
4. Pollution free	53%
5. Culture	51%
6. Parks	45%
23. Development	24%
23. Shopping	24%
28. Tourism	22%

Most frequent responses when asked for *machi zukuri* priorities:

1. Pleasant space	33%
2. Improved infrastructure	28%
3. Regional economic activity	17%

Source: Omuta City, "Yutakasa afureru machi zukuri" (Community Building with Overflowing Abundance), 1988.

The 1990 Public Opinion Survey

The uncertainty generated by these results prompted city officials to commission Kyūkechō to take another survey of local attitudes. Like the 1984 questionnaire, this one focused on development-oriented topics and offered closed-response options. Not surprisingly, it produced results skewed toward capital-intensive projects. Table 2 shows results largely consistent with those of the 1984 survey.

ANALYSIS OF SURVEY RESULTS

The three surveys and one election in the 1980s suggest bifurcated public opinion regarding Omuta's future. When prompted with closed-ended questions on economic development, residents listed their project preferences consistently. However, the open-ended questions indicate a strong interest in environmental issues that outweighed economic development concerns. As we shall see below in the list of projects attempted by the government, city officials undertook more economic development projects than environmental improvement efforts in their quest to revitalize Omuta.

Table 2. Omuta Public Opinion Survey Results, 1990

Things Omuta residents are lacking:	
Citizen unity	27%
Local patriotism	21%
Helpful spirit	26%
Omuta's most urgent need regarding facilities:	
Parking	43%
Higher education	29%
Sewers	28%
Advanced medical	23%
Art museum	22%

Source: Kyushu Economic Research Council, "Omuta shimin ishiki chōsa" (Survey of Omuta Residents' Attitudes), 1990.

It is unclear why city hall chose to emphasize concrete over greenery. The new mayor's Construction Ministry experience may provide a partial explanation, and national government programs made funds available for construction projects. Yet the Japanese government also had numerous programs for environmental improvement. Officials in city hall admitted taking their cues from other struggling cities. Omuta borrowed development ideas from cities throughout Japan, and anecdotal evidence suggests these efforts in other cities centered on economic development.

Interest-Group Activity

The collective voice of Omuta residents also sent conflicting and vague messages. Two main interest groups emerged to focus popular energy for revitalization in Omuta. These groups reflected the two-pronged agenda expressed in the survey results. They simultaneously called for economic development and for environmental improvement, but they were rather vague in expressing their ideas. Their main function seems to have been coordinating the expression of community sentiments for several different groups within the populace.

The first group to form was the Omuta Committee for Building a Pleasant Environment (Omuta-shi Kaiteki Kankyōzukuri Kyōgikai), which held its first meeting in 1987. The committee was a high-profile assembly of twenty-nine representatives from numerous organizations in the community. Representing a wide array of local interests (see table 3), the committee was an inclusive attempt to organize and mobilize citizen participation under one consensus-oriented mantle. In addition to representatives from the general public, two representatives from the Omuta city assembly and five from Omuta city hall also participated. Three prefectural bureaucrats and four academic specialists were also part of the group. The committee met three times over the next two years to discuss Omuta's development plans. Though it produced little in the way of concrete policy recommendations, it served as a communications mechanism for the government and the citizenry.

Table 3. Groups Represented on the Omuta Committee for Building a Pleasant Environment

Omuta Association of Elementary School PTAs
General Women's Union Council
Omuta Chamber of Youth
Omuta Chamber of Commerce and Industry
Mitsui Tōatsu Chemical, Omuta Plant
Bright Community-Building Promotion Committee
100,000 Tree Planting Promotion Committee
Omuta Citizens' Charter Planning and Promotion Committee
Omuta Tourism Council
Omuta Social Welfare Committee
Omuta Health Cooperative Union
Omuta Federation of Senior Citizens' Clubs
Omuta Federation of Handicapped Social Welfare Councils
Omuta Federation of Labor Unions
Ariake Labor Union Committee
Omuta Medical Association
Omuta City Planning Committee
Kyushu University
Fukuoka University
Omuta City Assembly (2)
Fukuoka Prefecture (3)
Omuta City Government (5)

The Omuta Ladies' 21 Steering Committee (Omuta Rediisu 21 Iinkai) was established in 1988. This group was made up of ten women ranging in age from nineteen to sixty-three. Like the Omuta Committee for Building a Pleasant Environment, they represented a range of community interests but were united by gender. Together with the Omuta Committee for a Pleasant Environment, they produced "Asu no Omuta o kangaeru" (Thinking about the Omuta of Tomorrow), a vague statement of goals for the future of Omuta. Topics covered included community building, tourism development, industrial development, environmental promotion, cultural development, transportation network improvement, and welfare improvement.[11] The report made no innovative policy suggestions, nor did it prioritize the issues listed. Instead, it was a catchall wish list ultimately authored by city hall bureaucrats.

The statement was useful from the perspective of local officials, however, since its generic and broad content made it an endorsement for any policies the government proffered. City officials could point to the document as validation for pursuing their own interests. Ironically, the lack of direction provided by local interest groups gave city hall bureaucrats a longer leash to work with.

Where are the traditional interest groups in Omuta? Where are the miners' labor unions? These organizations played marginal roles in Omuta's decision making in the 1980s. The legacy of defeat made union leadership in Omuta's revitalization unlikely. In addition to dramatic and violent defeats like the 1960 Miike Coal Mine dispute, local labor was ground down over three decades by a Mitsui-Omuta city government alliance. Every mayor prior to Shiotsuka came from within the Mitsui establishment and was elected with corporate support. Though national industrial rationalization policies provided a safety net for miners, the unions were unable to save jobs and maintain their organizational strength over time. The same labor groups that conducted the Miike strike lost most of their clout as the company cut jobs. Membership declined, and those that remained were older retired workers. The two regional labor union councils (The Omuta Federation of Labor Unions and the Ariake Labor Union Committee) had seats on the Omuta Committee for Building a Pleasant Environment, but the role they played was symbolic and peripheral.

Omuta's Government Shapes a New Future

Given the input from the community, what has Omuta done to catalyze renewed growth and confidence? Table 4 lists the seventeen projects con-

11. Ibid., 30-31.

tinued or started in Shiotsuka's first term as mayor. Two trends are evident from this list: first, only three of the seventeen projects are aimed at making Omuta a greener place to live; and second, the capital projects listed as desirable by the residents in surveys are not on this list.

Table 4. Redevelopment projects in Omuta, 1986–1992

Farm subsidies (cadmium problem)
Coal policy (continuing)
Ariake GeoBio World theme park
Downtown Area Activity Plan
   (Community Mart Model Project)
Kattachi Area Development Project
Omuta Zoo revitalization
Suwa Park Facilities Project
New City Hospital
Area road improvement
Industrial/regional promotion and corporate invitation
Omuta Central Industrial Park
Omuta Technopark Inland Industrial Park
   Development Project
Product distribution center
World Coal Technology Center
Miike Port facilities improvement plan
Central Ariake Region Activity Promotion Council
Ariake Coastal Summit

The Downtown Area Activity Plan, Omuta Zoo Revitalization, and Suwa Park Facilities Project all aimed to expand the green space in Omuta. The Downtown Area Activity Plan was a comprehensive shopping street (shōtengai) redevelopment plan that included the planting of trees and the creation of several pocket parks to improve the atmosphere. The Omuta Zoo was updated: trees were planted and an outdoor aviary was added. Suwa Park fit into the list of citizen preferences. The city purchased a piece of idle and contaminated industrial land from Mitsui, and they covered it with a thick two-meter layer of dirt. Grass was planted on the new soil, and lighted softball, baseball, and soccer fields were built. The city now has a major sports facility capable of hosting large tournaments for team sports.

Where are the facilities listed by the residents as most urgently needed? There are no plans to increase downtown parking, no improvements to higher-education facilities, no plans to expand the sewer system, no art museum, and no plans to raise the rail lines bisecting the heart of the city. Plans for a new hospital were under discussion, but they were still in the earliest stages and little hard data were available. Still, the city did actively work on the economic side of the residents' wish list. Plans were underway to upgrade the road network and port facilities. The most significant efforts during Shiotsuka's first term were industrial park development and attracting job-creating firms to Omuta. Three new industrial parks were created, and the city made a concerted effort to bring new businesses into Omuta.

The process of luring corporations (*kigyō yūchi*) began in 1980, well before the three projects described in the following paragraphs were up and running. Between 1980 and 1992, the city counted thirty-three successful cases of *kigyō yūchi*, most of which were achieved after 1986.[12] Thirty of the companies were involved in some sort of manufacturing, with seven in metals and/or ceramics, five in plastics, five in textiles, five in chemicals and fertilizers, and the remainder in service, food processing, or light manufacturing industries. Though thirty-three firms sounds impressive, the effect these companies have had on local employment statistics is marginal at best. Thirteen firms were already in existence in Omuta in some form, while twenty companies actually moved to Omuta from somewhere else. Only seven of the firms were Mitsui subsidiaries, but if one adds up Mitsui suppliers, the firms spun off from Mitsui concerns, and Mitsui subsidiaries—all the firms related to Mitsui and/or doing business with Mitsui concerns—the number grows to twelve. Firms related to Mitsui account for just over one-third of all *kigyō yūchi* in Omuta.

As of 1992, the Central Industrial Park housed four firms in just over 5 hectares of space. These firms employed 295 full-time workers.[13] The Central Industrial Park is a successful facet of redevelopment in Omuta. The city built and filled the park in four years and managed to attract firms from relatively clean industries while creating jobs for city residents. Though only 25% of the jobs were completely new hires, the park prevented two local firms looking for new quarters from moving elsewhere. Omuta's image as an industrial community—often cited as something residents want to change—even worked to its advantage. Omuta was able to beat out more rural towns in the competition for skilled factory production jobs.

12. This list excludes firms in the Product Distribution Center, which reinforce the trends observed in Omuta's *kigyō yūchi* in general.
13. Data provided by Omuta City Hall, Industrial Promotion Section.

The Omuta Product Distribution Center was completed and officially opened in April 1992. The job creation impact of the Product Distribution Center was moderate because most of the firms moving in were local. A total of 894 people were employed in the Center, of which 161 jobs were newly created. Though most of the firms that moved into the Product Distribution Center voiced an intent to hire even more employees, the nationwide economic slowdown in the early 1990s made this difficult. The center did add a new building in the fall of 1992 and found eight more firms to fill it. All were local; one was a Mitsui subcontractor, and one was a Mitsui subsidiary spun off as part of the companywide rationalization. The job impact of those firms was light: a total of 290 people were employed in the new addition, an additional 98 new jobs over pre-center employment levels. The Inland Industrial Park was only in its earliest planning stages when this research was conducted.

The impact of these industrial park efforts and general *kigyō yūchi* was minimal. Several hundred jobs were created over a ten-year period, but these were dwarfed by the cutbacks Mitsui made in its workforce.

To some extent, Omuta's policy choices did follow the citizens' stated preferences. Job creation and use of idle industrial land were obvious priorities for residents and for city hall officials. A few parks were created to expand the city's green space. However, as stated earlier, the vague, broad interests articulated by Omuta's citizens functionally gave the local government free rein to exercise almost any technocratic plans it produced. Indeed some of the projects on the city's list seem to have materialized out of nowhere, appearing on no list articulated by the public. The World Coal Technology Center and the GeoBio World theme park represent projects that were more supply-driven than demand driven. This suggests that there is still a fair amount of specialist policy-making in Japanese local economic development and intergovernmental relations. How did city officials come up with these ideas?

POLICY SPECIALISTS AND LOCAL ECONOMIC DEVELOPMENT

A common explanation for Japanese local government policy-making is that localities have limited local revenues and thus have limited decision-making freedom with respect to their annual budgets. The assumption is that money disbursed from the central government to a local government comes with strings attached—that the national government buys influence over local policy using financial incentives. Steven Reed points out that there is no necessary relationship between an entity's financial contribution and influence over policy. Simply put, influence over policy need not be proportional to financial contributions.[14]

A glance at Omuta's general budget figures for 1990 and 1991 in table 5 does little to support or refute this view. Omuta's finances look pretty much like those of its neighbors.[15] Its percentage of independent revenues (*jishu zaigen*) is comparable to other struggling cities. Areas with stronger economies have higher levels of revenue independence, but this is a marginal difference. Large-scale borrowing and manipulation of tax rates are not an option for local governments, since MOHA keeps a close eye on finances and enforces strict fiscal responsibility.

Cities like Omuta have only two ways to increase their revenues to finance new projects: by maximizing central grants and by setting up a formally private (often nonprofit) corporation.[16] Omuta did both, and in so doing was forced to partially sacrifice its own desires to take what the central government had to offer in the way of grants and aid.

Table 5. Omuta's Budget Data, 1990 and 1991 (in ¥100-man)

	1990	1991
Major general revenues		
Local taxes	13,753	14,213
Local allocation tax	10,936	11,338
Transfer tax	10,259	9,772
Local bonds	4,392	4,925
Total revenues	49,359	53,403
Major general expenditures		
Mandatory expenditures	24,526	25,016
Specified items	4,326	4,644
Transportation construction		
Grants	1,639	2,423
Independent projects	5,628	8,019
Unemployment policy allowance	1,649	1,673
Total expenditures	48,656	53,127

Source: Fukuoka-ken, "Shi-cho-son yōran," 1992.

14. Steven R. Reed, *Japanese Prefectures and Policymaking* (Pittsburgh: University of Pittsburgh Press, 1986), 14.
15. Fukuoka Prefecture, *Shi-cho-son yōran* (City-Town-Village Directory) (Fukuoka, 1992).
16. Reed, *Japanese Prefectures*, 27–32.

Using Policy Menus

When asked how they go about making urban redevelopment policy, Omuta's leaders often start by saying, "We look at the policy menu options offered by the various ministries, and we try to make our needs fit their goals." The World Coal Technology Center fits this description. Searching for a future, Omuta sent a study mission to Europe in October 1989—led by Mayor Shiotsuka—to see how communities in similar situations handled the decline of the coal industry. Upon their return, the mayor told the Japanese press that the British and West German governments took active measures to help unemployed workers find new jobs. This implied that the Japanese government did not do enough labor retraining and placement. In a ninety-five-page description, the mission reported its findings to the Energy Resources Agency (Shigen Enerugi-Cho, a branch of MITI) in Tokyo, and to other ministries and agencies as well. In it, they recommended the establishment of a World Coal Technology Center to study mine safety and other coal technology, to serve as a dissemination point for Japan's superior technical know-how to the other coal mining nations in the Asia-Pacific region, and to help promote the Omuta region.[17]

MITI quickly embraced this idea, and in December 1990 the first public meeting on the World Coal Technology Center was held in Omuta. Sponsored by MITI, it focused on three facets of the emerging plan: a coal technology research center, a mine safety center, and a pollution control research center. Officials from various MITI sections attended and served on the panel presenting the plan, along with representatives from the Japan Coal Association, the Coal Technology Development Cooperation Center, and Kyushu University.[18] Interestingly, no one from Mitsui Coal Mining presented a paper, and Mitsui Coal was not mentioned in any of the newspapers that day.

The World Coal Technology Center was a good example of Omuta playing the government structure skillfully. However, the project did not move forward quickly. On December 3, 1991, the Omuta city assembly announced its budget for the next fiscal year, including ¥13.8 million to study the World Coal Technology Center further. Half of this money came from MITI's "Special Coal Area Activity Project," one quarter was a grant from the prefecture, and the city put up the rest.[19] The good news was

17. *Asahi Shimbun*, October 31, 1989; *Yomiuri Shimbun*, March 10, 1990.
18. *Mainichi Shimbun*, December 21, 1990.
19. *Mainichi Shimbun*, December 3, 1991.

that the money was approved and allocated. The bad news was that the project was a long way from completion, but at least MITI was on board and supportive.

While this project was not intended to restore permanent jobs for Omuta's miners, it was aimed at providing construction jobs for the city. Furthermore, officials hoped to host visiting study groups from other Asian nations who would come to learn about Mitsui's advanced mining technology. This would create a few technical and scientific jobs in Omuta.

Copycat Policy-Making

As with many of Omuta's other projects, the city borrowed this idea from somewhere else. A similar mining technology research center (this one developed from a retired gold mine) was opened in Akita Prefecture in northern Honshu on February 20, 1992. Omuta officials do not see this other site as a competitor, and since such a center requires a preexisting mine facility, it is unlikely that the supply of mining research centers will outstrip the limited demand for mining research and development facilities. The *Facilities Planning Study Report* for the World Coal Technology Center devoted several pages to the Akita center, using it as an example of how to construct a similar facility in Omuta. The Akita center is a modest project, funded by MITI and built by Akita Prefecture at a cost of ¥1.2 trillion (roughly $12 million), that has research, training, and international exchange functions. The Omuta center looks like a virtual copy of its northern predecessor. It will consist of five buildings: a dormitory, restaurant, training center, institute for visiting graduate students, and coal industry data center. The total cost estimate for the first three buildings is ¥1.35 trillion (about $13.5 million).[20]

Nonprofit Public-Private Corporations

Omuta combined copycat policy-making with the nonprofit corporation strategy in developing the plan for its GeoBio World theme park. Theme parks were a popular economic development tool in the 1980s in Japan, and the spread of these facilities to the most rural regions is due entirely to policy diffusion supported by both local and national governments. However, Omuta started its theme park development efforts on the down

---

20. Overview of the *Facilities Planning Study Report* for the World Coal Technology Center, Omuta City, March 1992.

side of the "theme park boom," and thus had trouble generating government support for construction of the facility.

Tokyo Disneyland provided inspiration—or perhaps an idol—for GeoBio World planners. It inspired other park planners throughout Japan as well. The planning office walls in Omuta are sprinkled with Disney maps and posters, and souvenir dwarfs sit on the desks. The Tokyo park was mentioned several times in interviews with planning officials, and at one point they even hired some of Tokyo Disney's former ride designers to create attractions for the Omuta park.

In Japan, successful parks have not been owned and operated by large firms, as they are in the U.S. Except for Tokyo Disneyland, Japanese theme parks are relatively small mom-and-pop operations. Kitakyushu's Space World, Nagasaki's Holland Village and Huis Ten Bosch, Miyazaki's Sea Gaia, and other examples are each independent entities.

GeoBio World was pitched as the center piece of Omuta's redevelopment effort. It was planned and executed by Navel Land, Inc., a "third sector" (*daisan secta*) local development company established and capitalized jointly by the city of Omuta, Fukuoka Prefecture, and major companies from Omuta and the northern Kyushu region. Such public-private joint ventures were used in other Japanese theme parks. A similar company was established to build and manage Space World in Kitakyushu, for example. The name "Navel Land" was selected for three reasons: first, its end product—the GeoBio World theme park—was seen as the *heso jigyō* (literally, the "belly button project") in Omuta's revitalization plan, the project around which all others would revolve;[21] second, Omuta's history is focused on coal, a rock that comes from the belly of the earth; and third, Omuta is located in central Kyushu, and planners hoped to draw people from all over the island to the park.[22] The coal theme figured prominently in the park's attractions, and the development company sought to carry the theme from the mine to the opening of the tourist attraction.

Navel Land, Inc. was officially established in September 1989, with capital assets of ¥1.3 billion. The city started the capitalization ball rolling by committing ¥200 million in March 1989, and in April the city submitted a request for planning funds to the national government's Industrial Basic Facilities Fund (Sangyō Kiban Seibi Kikin), administered

21. While this sounds absurd by Western standards, the navel has strong positive connotations in Japanese culture. For example, some Japanese preserve the baby's umbilical cord, and shrines throughout Japan are devoted to the tie between mother and child. These shrines sell cakes (*heso manju*) celebrating the navel.
22. Explained by Hoshioka Morihiko, the first president of Navel Land, Inc., in an interview in the *Yomiuri Shimbun*, September 28, 1989.

by MITI. Fukuoka Prefecture matched the city with an additional ¥200 million in August of that year, and in September the city received a ¥200 million grant from the Industrial Basic Facilities Fund. Mitsui Mining and Mitsui Tōatsu Chemical contributed ¥200 million each, and the remaining ¥500 million came from Fukuoka Bank, Nishitetsu Railway Co., JR Kyushu, Kyushu Electric Power Co., and several other private sources.[23]

Navel Land was a firm with a narrow mission: the construction and management of GeoBio World. Company employees were provided on a two- or three-year personnel exchange basis (*jinji kōryū*) by city hall and the original investing companies. A senior management employee from one of the investing firms filled the company president's seat on a rotating basis. The first Navel Land President previously headed the Mitsui Tōatsu Chemical plant in Omuta.

Navel Land tried for years to finance and build GeoBio World. The Japan Development Bank (JDB) was the linchpin in the financing syndicate. The other capital sources—both public and private—agreed to finance the project, pending JDB approval of the Navel Land plan. But, for various reasons, the JDB rejected four plans. The JDB was involved in the Navel Land project from the earliest stages, and from the very first, it advised Omuta that it thought GeoBio World was a bad idea.[24] One of the biggest concerns was that there were already enough theme parks in northern Kyushu: Nagasaki is home to Holland Village and the newer Huis Ten Bosch; Spaceworld in Kitakyushu is quite close; and Mitsui Greenland in neighboring Arao (Kumamoto Prefecture) is a fifteen-minute taxi ride from Omuta Station. The competition was too fierce and the regional population not sufficient to support another theme park.

GeoBio World finally opened in July 1995 after eighteen months of construction. It cost just over $100 million to build, and expected attendance was 600,000 per year. Featured attractions included a simulation theater showing a four-minute film entitled "The Ultimate Roller Coaster," a coal industry science museum, an aquarium, and a botanical garden. The twelve-acre park (with a fifteen-acre parking lot) never came close to attendance projections, and it went bankrupt and closed less than two years after it opened. GeoBio World left Omuta with a per capita debt of ¥28,000, to be paid down over the years.

23. Interview with Sakaguchi Toshihide, Planning Section Chief at Navel Land, Inc. May 12, 1993; and Navel Land, Inc. report: "Neiburu rando ima made no keika" (The Development of Navel Land Up to Now), April 1993.
24. Interview with Ishii Kan, Planning Research Section Chief, Japan Development Bank, Fukuoka Branch, July 23, 1993.

CONCLUSION

Local economic redevelopment is a policy area where traditional characterizations of Japanese intergovernmental relations still apply. Revitalization efforts tend to be top-down, elite-led, and dominated by career civil servants. Governmental institutional structures and linkages reinforce these behavior patterns. Though citizen participation is rhetorically solicited by local elites, contributions by nonelites are peripheral at best. Overall, Japan's unitary system of government promotes a high degree of specialist-led policy-making for urban revitalization.

Omuta's bureaucrats and local leaders dominated policy-making. The mayor, a former Construction Ministry bureaucrat, worked to catalyze growth. City hall staff played a leading role in most of the projects attempted on his watch. They used limited public input to legitimate their policy decisions. This is not to say that officials were trying to exploit or dupe Omuta's residents. The bureaucrats truly had the city's best interests in mind, and they did their best to improve a difficult situation.

Despite these conclusions, the stereotype of "30% autonomy" does not accurately depict the state of center-local relations in urban revitalization efforts. Though roughly one-third of the city's redevelopment projects are funded at least in part with national money, the decision-making initiative for these projects clearly came from the local level. Local technocrats with a good understanding of the central finance system did their best to fit their needs into the policy menus offered by the central government agencies. Omuta's city government walked a fine line between doing what it wanted to do and doing what was feasible. This pattern allowed for a fair degree of local autonomy.

By the same token, Omuta's residents were highly visible but substantively marginalized in the policy process. Their opinions were solicited and their voices were heard, but few of their priorities made it onto the list of projects implemented. Those that did come to fruition were marginal in terms of their impact on the local economy. This may be due in part to the conflicting signals depicted in public opinion surveys. Residents wanted both economic growth and environmental sensitivity. They received little of the former and less of the latter.[25]

25. The author is grateful to the following individuals for their helpful comments and suggestions: John C. Campbell, Muto Yasukatsu, Imasato Shigeru, and Yamada Takato. I am grateful for financial support from Kyushu University and the University of Michigan.

Living in Harmony: Prospects for Cooperative Local Responses to Foreign Migrants

Katherine Tegtmeyer Pak

In 1987 ten nongovernmental organizations (NGOs) concerned with supporting foreign migrant workers living in Japan came together to form an umbrella organization known by the Japanese acronym Ajikon (shortened from Ajia Rōdōsha Mondai Kondankai, Round Table on the Asian Workers' Problem).[1] Their stated goal: "to join in actions building a Japanese society that could live in harmony with foreign migrant workers" (*ijū rōdōsha to kyōsei dekiru Nihon shakai*). Local governments in dozens of Japanese cities have professed virtually the same goal—of building "communities of harmonious living with foreigners" (*gaikokujin to no kyōsei shakai*).

Likewise, in their respective publications about international migration to Japan and the increased presence of foreigners in Japanese society, both NGOs and local governments relate their intentions to the cultural idiom of "internationalization" (*kokusaika*), and in particular, to the need for Japan to realize an "inward internationalization" (*uchi naru kokusaika*). The idea of inward internationalization suggests the possibility of breaching the boundaries of Japanese nationhood and moving beyond pressures for social and political homogeneity. In their interpretations, internationalization should lead to a more open, more flexible, and ultimately more democratic Japan.

Underlying these discussions of "harmonious living with foreigners" and "inward internationalization" is a critical stance toward the na-

1. I could not have written this article without the kind hospitality of the many NGOs that allowed me to attend their meetings and discussions. The members of Jōsei no Ie HELP, Nyūkan Mondai Chōsakai, and HLS no Kai were especially welcoming and encouraging of my research. I also owe thanks to Ann Kaneko, Joshua H. Roth, Matsuda Mizuho, and Professor Ebashi Takashi for providing key introductions. Ann Kaneko and Patricia Steinhoff made helpful comments on an earlier draft of this work. Finally, I gratefully acknowledge the Japan Foundation's financial support of the research presented here.

tional government's refusal to recognize Japan's emergence as a destination for international migration or to attempt to ensure that foreign migrants in Japan are not discriminated against. The national government's closure to the need for policies mediating between migrants and Japanese appears negligent to locally based actors who have witnessed first-hand the dramatic increase in the foreign population of Japanese cities. Local governments are filling part of that gap by recasting local internationalization projects to include "incorporation programs," which recognize foreign residents as "local citizens" (jūmin). NGOs, for their part, strive to help migrants solve any and all problems that befall them as legal and socio-cultural outsiders in Japanese society.

Despite the possibility of making common cause on this issue, the NGOs and local governments have yet to engage in much meaningful cooperation. Their struggles to initiate programs that peacefully incorporate migrants into Japanese society coexist in parallel but separate local contexts. To an outside observer, both parties seem likely to benefit from cooperating, since they might then present a unified counterweight, reflecting local conditions and needs, to the national government's position on immigration-related issues. Why then hasn't such a partnership ensued? Two factors have impeded NGOs and local governments from cooperating to achieve the shared goal of increased openness in Japanese society.

First, their understanding of what problems are created by immigration differ. Additionally, even though local government and NGOs use a common rhetoric at the most general level, their interpretations of what is required to put the rhetorical goals into practice diverge at important points. The NGOs are much harsher in their assessments of how migrants are treated in Japan, by the government, their employers, and the public at large. Negative experiences of individual migrants are deployed as emblems of the suffering and exploitation that NGOs believe face all non-Western migrants in Japan. Their version of a Japanese society in "harmony" with foreign migrants denies the relevance of visa status or citizenship in the application of Japanese social services and labor laws. Local governments, by contrast, place more emphasis on the need to ensure that cultural differences between foreign migrants and Japanese do not lead to "misunderstandings" on either side. They are worried that immigration will cause the kinds of urban "ghettoization," unrest, and violence experienced in European cities with large foreign populations. Moreover, as governments are wont to do, they tend to be more concerned with statistical or systemic trends than migrants' individual experiences. And although the local government interpretation of "harmonious" local communities clearly de-emphasizes national citizenship as a prerequisite for community membership and even access to social ser-vices, it does not envision extending that membership to undocumented migrants. Migrants are generally expected to be in compliance with all Japanese laws, including the immigration statutes, before local govern-ments are willing to extend the state benefits that they manage.[2]

Second, the marginal institutional position of NGOs in Japanese politics hinders cooperation between them and local government. The NGOs supporting foreign migrants usually do not have any formal legal status. They are typically small and overwhelmingly dependent upon volunteers. They are not part of mainstream electoral politics. Further-more, they are usually new groups, formed only since the increased in-ternational migration to Japan in the 1980s. Consequently, local govern-ments often do not have much information about their existence or agen-das. These characteristics do not make them the most attractive part-ners for local bureaucrats, who find it easier to cooperate through ongo-ing relationships with stable organizations. Nor do the NGOs relish co-operating with local government. Their dislike of legalistic, bureaucratic approaches to the human problems they encounter in supporting mi-grants is compounded by their suspicions that local government would like to co-opt them. Accepting financial assistance from local govern-ment is therefore usually seen as a dubious strategy, since it is expected to entail adoption of bureaucratic procedures and priorities. Recent na-tional government attempts to bring unincorporated NGOs into a for-mal registration system have heightened activists' apprehensions that government actors are trying to control their organizations. In sum, the weakness of the NGO sector in Japanese politics fuels an atmosphere of mistrust between its participants and local government, which must be overcome for any concrete cooperation to occur.

Still, the possibility for cooperation exists. It is discussed inde-pendently by the NGOs and local governments themselves and encour-aged by intellectuals with ties to both communities. The themes of "in-ternationalization" and "harmonious co-existence" may not be inter-preted isomorphically, but there is enough shared content to warrant analysis of the prospects for increased contacts, growing mutual respect, and ultimately policy cooperation between the NGO sector and local governments in their efforts to respond to the growing foreign popula-tion in Japan.

2. Two laws pertain: the Immigration Control and Refugee Recognition Act (Shutsu Nyūkoku Kanri oyobi Nanmin Nintei Hō) and the Alien Registration Law (Gaikokujin Tōroku Hō).

This chapter approaches the question of NGO–local government cooperation by focusing on the agendas and activities of the NGOs. It first outlines the emergence of this new category of citizens' group in Japan and discusses their ongoing coalescence into a national movement with a nascent political agenda. Next is a review of the institutional position of Japanese NGOs in general, which supports my argument that their vulnerability compromises their capacity to affect immigration-related policies. Finally I will discuss the growing interest in connecting NGO and local government initiatives into a type of community-based response to international migration.

Participants in Local Internationalization

Rapidly increasing international migration captured the attention of the Japanese public in the late 1980s. In the first decade of this trend, from 1984 to 1994, the number of foreigners registered as resident in Japan increased by more than 60%. Concurrently, the number of foreigners living illegally in Japan rose from several thousand to over 300,000. Despite the intense spotlight cast upon these developments by the mass media and the intellectual community, Japanese political parties and politicians have not politicized immigration as have their counterparts in other advanced industrial democracies. Debates over immigration issues, instead of taking place in the electoral arena, occur largely within a framework constructed by the Japanese bureaucracy. Nationally, the Ministry of Justice has struggled, with only partial success, to keep economic interests in increased labor migration from compromising its postwar exclusionary stance on immigration.

Locally, in contrast, many prefectural and municipal governments have decided to take it upon themselves to move beyond exclusion, to mediation of interactions between their Japanese constituents and the growing foreign population.[3] Many different departments within city government deal with foreign migrants: among them, health, education, housing, and labor officials. The local bureaucrats behind the plans to create "harmonious communities with foreigners," however, are

---

3. Not all local governments have made this decision, and there are significant differences even between those that have decided to craft incorporation policies. I discuss these differences in detail in a study of four cities (Kawasaki, Shinjuku, Kawaguchi, and Hamamatsu) in "Foreigners Are Local Citizens, Too: Local Governments Respond to International Migration in Japan," in Mike Douglass and Glenda S. Roberts, eds., *Japan and Global Migration: Foreign Workers and the Advent of a Multicultural Society* (London: Routledge, 2000).

assigned to "international offices." Funding for the creation of these of-fices was made available by the Ministry of Home Affairs, in the 1980s, to manage passive internationalization projects such as sister city and cultural exchange events. International offices were not intended to be-come the base for incorporating foreign migrants. Since the growth in foreign population coincided with their creation, however, local bureau-crats who had previously launched tentative efforts reaching out to for-eigners were able to redefine local internationalization to include such initiatives. In doing so, they have broadened the scope of programs un-der their jurisdiction and thus the importance of their own positions.[4]

Local bureaucrats' crafting of incorporation policies are based in the history of their cities. Community members thus often provided the initial catalyst for the policies, but bureaucrats are largely defining the policy agendas themselves, in relative isolation from politicians, po-litical parties, local businesses, and even citizens' groups. Though the first three groups of potential partners in local government's efforts have ex-pressed little interest in the issue, there are small citizens' groups in most cities with significant migrant populations that profess similar goals of incorporation.

Although I refer to them as nongovernmental organizations (NGOs) in this paper, there is neither a single definition nor even a single term that describes all of the private organizations assisting foreign mi-grants in Japan.[5] Some of the organizations refer to themselves as NGOs, but perhaps because this English acronym tends to connote an overseas development or cooperation agenda in the Japanese context,[6] others are uncomfortable describing themselves in this way. Most groups willingly describe themselves in general terms as *shimin dantai* (citizens' organi-zations), or more specifically as *gaikokujin rōdōsha* (or *ryūgakusei*) *shien dantai* (foreign workers'/student support organizations). Since 1996, the most politicized of the organizations have deliberately and self-con-

---

4. Tegtmeyer Pak, "Foreigners Are Local Citizens, Too."
5. I choose to use NGOs to refer to these organizations because it is broad enough to en-compass both the support groups and labor unions. I favor NGO over "citizens' organi-zation" because the latter might suggest that the activities are limited to Japanese citi-zens. Although the majority of participants in these organizations are Japanese citi-zens, there are foreign migrants participating in some of them, and in fact, most of the organizations invite such participation.
6. Menju Toshihiro and Aoki Takako, "Japan: The Evolution of Japanese NGOs in the Asia Pacific Context," in Yamamoto Tadashi, ed., *Emerging Civil Society in the Asia Pacific Community* (Tokyo: Japan Center for International Exchange, 1996), and Ito Michio, "Tenkanki no NGO katsudo: rekishi to tenbo," in Watado Ichirō, ed., *Jichitai seisaku no tenkai to NGO* (Tokyo: Akashi Shoten, 1996).

sciously moved away from that terminology in favor of *ijū rōdōsha shien dantai* (migrant worker support organizations), which emphasizes their radical position in Japanese discourse on immigration.[7] Most of the organizations are heavily, if not solely, dependent on volunteers, although several of the best-known groups, with ties to the religious or professional community (such as Jōsei no Ie HELP, LAFLR/Gaikokujin Rōdōsha Bengodan), are able to maintain small paid staffs.

The Catholic Church and activists involved in transnational campaigns against prostitution were the first Japanese groups to address the concerns of foreign migrants. In response, activists such as the Asian Women's Association redirected earlier campaigns against Japanese sex tourism into programs to help women who began coming to work in Japan in the early 1980s. The Catholic Bishops' Conference of Japan established in 1983 a special committee, Solidarity Group with Migrant Workers in Japan, to encourage Japanese dioceses to respond to migrant women's needs by providing staff for counseling, masses in foreign languages, shelters, and so forth.[8] These diocesan groups have also been instrumental in organizing volunteers and providing information to the mass media. The Japan's Women's Christian Temperance Union (J-WCTU), a Protestant coalition that has campaigned against prostitution in Japan for decades, provides financial support and facilities for Jōsei no Ie HELP, a women's shelter in Tokyo. HELP, like these other organizations, mobilized preexisting agendas, domestic and transnational contacts, and political strategies to the nascent efforts to support foreign migrants.

In addition to these experienced activists, many small, local NGOs were started in the late 1980s in direct response to the new international migration to Japan. Those organizations formed specifically to respond to the "newcomers" generally frame migration as an issue of human rights and Japanese relations with Asia. Another group of NGOs is comprised of small, radical labor unions: for example, the Edogawa Union (Edogawa Yunion), the Foreigner Labor Union—General National

7. The language is "radical" because the Japanese language terms for migrant and immigration are typically not used. In the case of the national government, this choice of rhetoric signals a commitment to a homogeneous Japanese nation in which immigration and the presence of migrants are inconceivable. The NGOs thus use the term *ijū rōdōsha* to highlight their belief that Japan has irrevocably become a country of immigration. Strategic attempts to reframe the terms defining political issues are a common component of NGO activities throughout the world and across issues. See Margaret E. Keck and Kathryn Sikkink, *Activists Beyond Borders: Advocacy Networks in International Politics* (Ithaca: Cornell University Press, 1998).

8. Asian Women's Association, *Women from across the Seas: Migrant Workers in Japan* (Tokyo: Asian Women's Association, 1988).

Labor Tokyo Branch (FLU Zenrōkyō), or the Kanagawa City Union (Kanagawa Shiitii Yunion). These groups, originally established to advocate the rights of workers in Japan's peripheral labor market, see foreign migrants as fellow exploited workers shut out from the formally generous protection of Japanese labor laws by social prejudice, by their own lack of knowledge about the system, and, in the case of undocumented migrants, by their lack of the proper visa status. These three types of organizations form the core community of those Japanese attempting to ensure that foreigners living and working in Japan are protected from various forms of exploitation, harassment, and prejudice.[9]

The total number of NGOs active in this field is difficult to ascertain, in part because of the difficulty in drawing strict boundaries of activity, but also because many groups operate under such tenuous financial and organizational circumstances that they dissolve and reform in short periods of time. These limited resources also prevent some organizations from participating in national networks, and thus from being counted in efforts to maintain such a list.[10] My 1996 review of subscribers to the *Ijū rōdōsha tsūshin*, published by the Ajikon network, generated a list of 125 organizations that appeared to be migrant support group NGOs of some kind. Regional and national forums held in April each year since 1992 have brought together increasingly larger numbers of activists—a 1996 forum, although held in Fukuoka, quite far from the eastern Japan cities with the largest concentration of groups supporting migrants, had more than 400 people in attendance, representing perhaps sixty different organizations.

9. Other organizations sympathetic to the human rights-Asian relations perspective on international migration to Japan may not see resolution of these problems as a defining goal, yet nonetheless they provide peripheral support to the core organizations. Japanese branches of international NGOs such as Amnesty International fall into this category. Small neighborhood-based groups of volunteer Japanese language teachers are other potential supporters. Likewise, organizations initially established as part of the movement among Zainichi Koreans to improve their standing in Japanese society tend to be interested in the activities of the NGOs supporting "newcomer" migrants (newcomer being the Japanese term distinguishing recent migrants from "oldcomer" Koreans).

10. Published lists of these NGOs underestimate their numbers: for example, the *1994 NGO Directory* prepared by the NGO Katsudō Suishin Sentaa lists forty-four organizations active in the human rights field, which they define to include groups supporting foreign migrants, and an additional twelve organizations that support foreign refugees (reported in Ito, "Tenkanki no NGO katsudo," 308). In 1992, the Osaka Bar Association listed sixty-nine organizations in its "Directory of Groups Supporting Foreigners in Japan" (Ōsaka Bengoshikan, *Human Rights Handbook for Foreigners in Japan* [Tokyo: Akashi Shoten, 1992]).

COOPERATION BETWEEN LOCAL ACTORS

Support for foreign migrants in Japan is very much locally based, whether provided by local government or activists. Local governments do keep abreast of developments in other localities and tend to judge their own programs against those in other cities and prefectures.[11] They are able to do so in several ways. One example is research that is conducted by one locality regarding its own programs and then is distributed to other localities nationwide. Other reports directly compare developments throughout Japan.[12] The Ministry of Home Affairs (MOHA) provides other outlets for local bureaucrats to exchange information on making incorporation programs the focus of local internationalization. Their seminars and symposia on internationalization topics give bureaucrats formal and informal opportunities to discuss these issues with their peers in other cities. *Jichitai kokusaika fōramu* (Local Government Internationalization Forum), a magazine published by MOHA affiliate Jichitai Kokusaika Kyōkai and distributed to all local governments, features stories about internationalization efforts in different cities, including reports of some of the more original and possibly contentious initiatives. Finally, some municipal government officials often exchange information with their counterparts within the same prefecture, again through opportunities provided by seminars or longer symposia.

Despite multiple avenues for sharing information, there is virtually no substantive cooperation between localities on this issue. Nor do local governments yet sustain cooperation with NGO activists in their own cities, in most cases. With sufficient resources at hand for initial attempts to frame incorporation programs, it seems that they have not needed to reach out to the activist community. Many of their initiatives rely upon volunteers from the community, but there are apparently enough individuals (many of them housewives or retirees) not affiliated with NGOs to keep them in operation.

As for NGO members, since they are generally committed to solving the problems that face migrants living in their particular community, they care about how local socioeconomic factors affect migrants'

---

11. Of course this is true of other policy issues as well. See Steven R. Reed, *Japanese Prefectures and Policymaking* (Pittsburgh: University of Pittsburgh Press, 1986), and Richard J. Samuels, *The Politics of Regional Policy in Japan: Localities Incorporated?* (Princeton: Princeton University Press, 1983) for other examples of information flows between local governments.

12. Tokyo-to Seikatsu Bunkakyoku Kokusaibu, *Kokunai jichitai no kokusaika shisaku chōsa: kokunai 29 jijitai* (Tokyo: Seikatsu Bunkakyoku Kokusaibu, 1994).

experiences. Even NGOs created by religious organizations with experience in transnational advocacy campaigns have focused their efforts on specific localities.[13] Yet, NGO members have generally been fairly unconcerned with the local political environment. They are not tied into local party politics or connected with city or prefectural politicians. Consequently, as they have started to expand their activities from the day-to-day business of counseling individuals, their impulse for building networks has been to build them horizontally, within the activist community rather than their geographical community. Their political energies are directed into constructing a national social movement rather than partnerships with local actors unaffiliated with NGOs.

This horizontal networking has been successful enough that NGOs now comprise a community of shared political opinion, even though most of them have been in operation for little more than a decade. This is not to imply that they are a homogenous political grouping[14] but rather to point out that sharing informational resources has provided them with a shared political rhetoric and a set of common goals. Given their limited resources, the NGOs have made remarkable progress in consolidating a national network. The networks rely upon participation in regular gatherings such as the National Forum held each April, organization of joint committees to address specific issues such as health care for undocumented migrants, and exchange of the newsletters that NGOs produce to circulate to their own members.

Ties between NGOs were first formed within geographic regions as activists reached out to neighboring groups to share information about immigration law and expertise on how best to resolve the problems encountered in particular cases. Personal ties between individual activists with previous experience in social movements provided a foundation for network building. Preexisting institutions in the broader activist community, such as the Pacific Asia Resource Center (Ajia Taiheiyō Shuryō Sentaa, or PARC), provided a forum for their efforts to contact others with similar agendas sympathetic to foreign migrants.[15] Cooperative relationships with religious organizations (Catholic and Protestant) also greatly

13. The term "transnational advocacy" is from Keck and Sikkink, *Activists beyond Borders*.
14. Glenda S. Roberts, "NGO Support for Migrant Labor in Japan," in Douglass and Roberts, *Japan and Global Migration*, details the differences amongst the NGOs by comparing the operation of a set of labor unions and women's shelters dealing with undocumented foreign migrants in the Tokyo area. Her focus on how feminist ideology and attention to the effects of gender on migrants' experiences in Japan distinguishes the women's shelters from other NGOs is particularly useful.
15. Ōsaka Bengoshikai, *Human Rights Handbook*.

facilitated initial NGO networking.[16] Similar preexisting ties between small labor unions have also proven valuable resources for networking among supporters of migrants.

At the 1997 session of the National Forum on Migrant Workers' Issues, NGO activists spelled out their plans for a formally organized national network.[17] The network is to maintain offices in the Japan Council of Churches headquarters in Tokyo (the same as Ajikon). It is intended to institutionalize existing patterns of information exchange, to take over the planning of the annual National Forum from the ad hoc committees that had been doing it, to coordinate lobbying efforts, to foster transnational networking, and generally to seek to influence public opinion in Japan.

RHETORICAL GOALS AND PRACTICAL AGENDAS

Over the past decade local governments and NGOs have developed their interpretations of the significance of international migration for Japanese society. Although both sets of actors identify the need for harmonious interaction between foreign migrants and Japanese citizens as their overarching goal, the scope of interventions to which they aspire are quite different. This is reflected in the content of their agendas. The source of these differences is largely attributable to their institutional identities: NGOs may be characterized as "principled activists" engaging in moralistic campaigns, while local bureaucrats are concurrently public servants of local communities and, of course, agents of the Japanese state, with all of the accompanying legal constraints. The following review of each actor's interpretation of local internationalization and the agendas it has set reveals significant differences. However, the review also shows that there are some overlapping activities that might allow for meaningful cooperation.

NGOs tend to frame international migration in terms of exploitation. Their statements of broad ideological goals like internationalization and harmonious living with foreigners rest upon concrete actions

---

16. Ajikon, mentioned in the introduction, exemplifies the importance of these older activist and religious organizations in fostering the NGO community supporting migrants. PARC played a critical role in initiating the group (author communication with Ann Kaneko, March 1998). Their offices are provided by the Japan Council of Churches (Nihon Kirisutokyō Kyōgikai, or NCC), and when Ajikon faced budget deficits in 1994, a Christian constituent group (Nanmin/Gaikokujin Rōdōsha Mondai Kirisutosha Renrakukai) provided loans to tide them over.
17. As reported in HLS no Kai *Newsletter*, no. 76, June 1997.

intended to alleviate that exploitation. Moral righteousness and passion closely link practice and discourse in NGO activism. Whether in organizational meetings, public symposia, or their writings, these groups connect larger ideological themes to particular events by emphasizing the human drama to be found in problems faced by foreign migrants. To borrow a phrase, NGO members are "principled activists" whose activism brings ideas of harmonious living and human rights to life.[18] Personal experience in assisting individual migrants supports the conviction of NGO activists that Japanese society persistently discriminates against foreigners, especially those who are not from North America or Europe.[19] Immigration law is in their view the institutionalization of Japan's exclusionary social tendencies, an attempt by the government to use visa status and citizenship to prevent migrants from realization of the innate human rights due all individuals and from having protection under Japanese labor laws, which apply to all workers in Japan irrespective of visa status or nationality. NGOs present themselves as altruistically motivated seekers of justice, free of the self-interest and prejudice that motivate other actors (primarily government agencies and employers) who shape migrants' experiences in Japan.

Moral righteousness informs their attitudes toward the idiom of internationalization, such that any invocation of it is qualified to show

18. The quoted phrase is from Keck and Sikkink's discussion of transnational advocacy networks. They point out that "practices [of activists] do not simply echo norms—they make them real. Without the disruptive activity of these actors neither normative change nor change in practices is likely to occur" (*Activists beyond Borders*, 35).

19. This tendency by NGOs to generalize from individual cases of exploitation in their arguments about Japanese society's discrimination toward migrants alienates some other actors interested in migration issues. For example, one professor with research ties to the small manufacturers who use migrant labor wearily emphasized to me that a few spectacular cases of abuse notwithstanding, most businesses employing foreign migrants were not mistreating them. Indeed, my interviews with employers and informal discussions with migrants revealed that there are many instances of generally positive employer/worker relations where both sides are happy with their arrangement. There are also cases of outright friendship between employers and undocumented workers, where both parties feel a close alliance in their "illegal" labor transaction's contravention of immigration statutes. The documentary film *Overstay* (1998), directed by Ann Kaneko, portrays the actual complexity and diversity in the relationships between undocumented foreign migrants and Japanese society. Although there is not sufficient evidence to judge the overall experiences of migrants in Japan, there is enough to support NGO claims of multiple legal and social barriers against foreigners. In *Gaikokujin rōdōsha kenri hakushō*, the small unions supporting foreign workers in the Tokyo metropolitan area list 339 incidents, involving 641 foreign workers, over the course of fiscal year 1993, of wage, dismissal, work injury, and so on. where they were asked to represent the workers in their claims. Further systematic research on the daily working environment faced by migrants would be very valuable.

that NGOs are seeking a "true" or "real" internationalization that entails fundamental changes in Japanese society. Questioned about the goals of their organization, they respond with rhetoric claiming authenticity:

> [Our goals are to] treat our fellow Asians as human beings, end prejudice and discrimination, realize a society that appreciates other countries' culture and customs—true international exchange and mutual understanding.[20]

These claims of authenticity are implicitly targeted against what they see as the vague and self-serving nature of internationalization programs promoted by government authorities, as demonstrated in the response of another NGO to the same question:

> We strive for a society where all people can receive health care inexpensively, regardless of their nationality, philosophy, beliefs, or religion. This is clearly related to the support of foreigners and to problems in Japanese society. The Nagano Olympics are being promoted by the government as proof of Japan's internationalization, but such internationalization is limited to insincere overtures to North Americans and Europeans and is unrelated to daily life. Real internationalization would reach out to the foreigners who actually live in this area and would ensure that we are living in daily harmony with them.[21]

Local governments, however, see immigration as a problem due to its potential to disrupt the social and cultural stability of their communities.[22] They reach out to migrants in order to prevent cultural differences from leading to "mutual misunderstandings."[23] Rhetoric about their approaches to migrants is typically less moralistic and often en-

---

20. The question was asked as part of a mail survey conducted by the author with cooperation from Jōsei no Ie HELP. The survey was sent in January 1996 to 131 organizations; responses were received from 42 of them, for a response rate of 32%. Respondent #37.
21. Respondent #121.
22. This does not mean that local bureaucrats individually are unconcerned with migrants being exploited. Many bureaucrats that I interviewed were indeed aware of exploitation but saw it as falling outside their jurisdiction. For example, bureaucrats working in different international offices mentioned problems with unpaid wages as a responsibility for branch offices from the Ministry of Labor; questions of prostitution as a problem to be dealt with by the police, and migrant interest in more educational opportunities as ultimately falling to the discretion of the Board of Education. The most active international offices do try to connect these issues across jurisdictional boundaries through research reports and special committees.
23. Tegtmeyer Pak, "Foreigners Are Local Citizens, Too."

visages a less dramatic change to Japanese society. The following quote explaining why Shinjuku surveyed its foreign residents shows a more dispassionate interpretation of internationalization:

> In order to consider the ways in which to develop administrative services and a local society that correspond to internationalization, we aim to ascertain the extent to which foreigners residing in the city: interact with Japanese; face obstacles within their daily lives; are aware of city policies, and participate in various exchange events.[24]

Individual bureaucrats may see a need for Japanese society to change in light of this issue, even if official pronouncements in their cities do not acknowledge the same. An official in Kawaguchi evaluated his city's fairly limited incorporation program in language that echoed that of NGOs: "If it were real internationalization, then we would like to do more [for migrants] in the area of education."[25] "Internationalization is exactly this point," a Hamamatsu official explained to me, "that we can no longer continue doing things according to Japanese common sense. We need to come up with new rules."[26] But even when they think that Japan must change to accommodate foreigners, bureaucrats are generally more interested in issues of how migration affects Japanese than are NGO activists.

Different perspectives on what kinds of problems are involved in migration obviously affect the agendas of the two sets of local actors. For both local government and NGOs, however, providing information that helps individual migrants solve their problems is the most basic activity. Local governments have focused on overcoming language barriers. Maps, information about the city and its government offices, community newsletters, and guides to daily life in Japan are increasingly available in an ever wider range of foreign languages. Japanese language classes are taught free or at minimal expense in public community centers. Consultation services in foreign languages are available in person and over the telephone, with migrants seeking assistance most frequently for problems involving their employers, health care, family law issues, residency status, and immigration procedures.

NGOs offer assistance with the same range of issues, also through some combination of telephone and face-to-face consultations. But their

---

24. Shakai Kagaku Kenkyūjo, *Shinjuku-ku no kokusaika ni muketa shisaku taikei seibi ni tomonau chōsa kenkyū hōkokushō* (Tokyo: Shinjuku-ku Sōmubu, Heiwa/Kokusai Kōryū Tantō, 1992), 23.

25. Interview November 27, 1995.

26. Interview July 17, 1995.

advisory efforts differ from those of local governments in two important ways. First, they are more likely to follow an issue through to its resolution, while government programs frequently advise a person by answering questions in one session and then introducing them to other relevant bureaucratic offices, or even to NGOs if further assistance is necessary. NGOs often virtually adopt particular individuals, going with them to government offices as necessary, arranging for legal assistance and translators, providing shelter for women trying to escape forced prostitution, confronting recalcitrant employers at the workplace for back wages or compensation for injury, and even providing funds for health care or tickets home.[27] Second, NGOs offer their consultation services to all foreign migrants regardless of their legal status. Local governments, however, will usually only work with foreigners who are legally resident in Japan.[28]

This highlights another important difference between the two kinds of local actors. As agents of the Japanese state, local governments are required to uphold all Japanese laws, including immigration laws. NGOs, however, deny that visa status or citizenship should be seen as appropriate qualifications for the resolution of these various problems. The quest for harmony between Japanese and non-Japanese means that all persons living in Japan should be able to expect equal access to the social protection provided by the Japanese state.[29] They offer multiple justifications for that belief: pragmatically phrased arguments that mi-

27. Clearly there are plenty of cases where NGO assistance is also limited to one instance of advising with little follow through. Very few NGOs are able to do all of these things on their own, and by no means do all migrants seeking assistance require all of these forms of support. When a single NGO does encounter someone who needs wide-ranging help, however, they will seek additional support from fellow NGOs if the original group does not have enough resources to manage the case on its own.

28. I say "usually" here because this is something that is more likely to be understood than stated outright. That is, local governments are unlikely to have formalized restrictions on the provision of information to undocumented foreigners, even though they are expected to report such persons to national authorities for deportation proceedings. Most undocumented foreigners are thought (by local government and NGOs alike) to avoid government officials of their own accord. Yet there is always the chance that undocumented migrants receive help from government offices from time to time. This seems likely in light of some undocumented migrants' practice of actually registering as foreign residents with local government (*gaikokujin tōroku*) in order to gain ID cards, without being reported to immigration authorities.

29. For more on the development of similar beliefs—that all persons are entitled to equal protection from all states, regardless of their formal citizenship—in the United States and Western Europe, see David Jacobson, *Rights across Borders: Immigration and the Decline of Citizenship* (Baltimore: Johns Hopkins University Press, 1996) and Yasemin Nuhoglū Soysal, *Limits of Citizenship: Migrants and Postnational Membership in Europe* (Chicago: University of Chicago Press, 1994).

gration is an inevitable economic force; appeals to universal standards of human rights; appeals to the commonality of interest between all laborers; vaguely contradictory anti-racist calls for pan-Asian fellowship; and belief in Christian principles of loving one's fellow man. In short, NGOs deny the legitimacy and challenge the efficacy of Japanese immigration law. The relationship between pragmatism and deeper beliefs is captured in the following discussion of the moral poverty of Japanese immigration statutes:

> [These immigration reforms], by trying to use legal barriers to stop the flow of people, ignore the reality that the workers have no choice but to come and work in Japan, that the excessive economic disparities between Japan and the Asian regions cause inevitable labor flows. This reform would go even further in treating foreign workers as criminals and would clearly result in entrapping them in the detrimental condition of "illegality." Already it is difficult for them to receive care when ill or injured at work; already they are compelled to accept either having their wages skimmed or not being paid at all. Yet this reform would worsen an already bad situation by further trampling upon their human rights. . . . The problem of foreign workers will never be resolved through strengthening detention and exclusion practices. Rather, we should seek long-term building of international economic relations, which would make it unnecessary for them to migrate for work. In the meanwhile, we should quickly adopt policies that treat those workers who must come as human beings and workers whose rights are protected.[30]

Lobbying for policy change is a second category of locally based action intended to foster harmonious relations between foreign migrants and Japanese. Local governments and NGOs both include certain policy changes among their goals and on their practical agendas, though the changes they publicly argue for are not the same. The most notable lobbying efforts of local governments are related more to the plight of Zainichi Koreans. Migrants to Japan during its colonial rule of Korea and their descendants, the Zainichi hold permanent residency status but continue to face legal and social discrimination. Hundreds of local govern-

---

30. The quote, from a *Kalabaw no Kai* letter appealing for opposition to the 1989 reform to the Immigration Control and Refugee Recognition Act, was published as the preface in the seventh volume of their widely distributed collection of newspaper clippings related to foreign migrants, March 1989.

ments have supported campaigns to gain local voting rights and the right to work in local administration by petitioning the national government.[31]

NGOs recognized the need to include lobbying efforts on their agendas with the national government's move to reform the Immigration Control and Refugee Recognition Act in 1989. Opposing the revision's crackdown on undocumented migration for the reasons cited in the previous quote, NGOs argued instead that the national government should issue an amnesty for all migrants then working illegally in Japan.[32] The question of health care for uninsured foreigners has been another target of NGO lobbying efforts. Petitions protesting the Ministry of Health and Welfare's December 1991 decision to deny insurance coverage to undocumented migrants were sent by NGOs across Japan.[33] The appeal was also extended to local governments, who were requested to apply old, unused provisions from the "Treatment of Ill Travelers Law" to justify coverage of uninsured migrants, to expand eligibility for national health insurance to foreigners on short-term visas, and to implement other changes in national health insurance programs.[34] Fierce opposition to the Immigration Bureau's detention and deportation operations has provided a third topic for NGO lobbying activities. The 1994 death of an Iranian man while in the custody of the Immigration Bureau led to the creation of an umbrella NGO (Nyūkan Mondai Chōsakai) uniting attorneys, members of other NGOs, and journalists.[35] Under the guidance of that group, which has become a clearinghouse for claims of physical and sexual assault by Immigration Bureau staff, the combined NGO effort has been impressive. Its credibility is so high and its findings of a pattern of abuse are so serious that with two Diet members' facilitation it successfully arranged

31. See also the articles in the July 1992 special issue of *Toshi Mondai*.
32. See the preface to the *Kalabaw no Kai* newspaper collection from September 1989 (vol. 10). Calls for amnesty have been subsequently featured at the Regional and National Forums that meet every April. At the first Forum (1991) held for the Kanto region, a Pakistani migrant in attendance entreated the NGOs to think about changing the legal status of undocumented migrants, arguing that this would be of much greater assistance than series of support drives (*Kalabaw no Kai*, vol. 19, March 1991, preface). HLS no Kai *Newsletter*, no. 36, June 1, 1993, reports on the amnesty debate at the Third Forum (1993). The call for amnesty was also included in the "Fukuoka Appeal" issued at the end of the Sixth Forum (1996).
33. An alliance of NGOs from Kanagawa took the lead in mobilizing this campaign. The Kanagawa group itself collected more than 12,000 signatures for this petition drive. See the preface to the *Kalabaw no Kai* collection, vol. 24, March 1992.
34. Campaigns on this issue by an alliance of Shizuoka NGOs are reported in HLS no Kai *Newsletter*, no. 25, July 1, 1992. The Kanagawa alliance's campaign is discussed in the preface to *Kalabaw no Kai*, vol. 26, July 1992.
35. Nyūkan Mondai Chōsakai, *Misshi no jinken shingai: Nyūkan kanri kyoku shuyo shisetsu no jittai* (Tokyo: Gendai Jinbunsha, 1996).

two deliberative meetings with officials from the Immigration Bureau.[36] Given the absence of freedom of information legislation in Japan and any corresponding requirement that bureaucrats respond directly to citizens' groups, as opposed to citizens' representatives in the Diet, this is a substantial achievement. It is that much more impressive because there was no precedent for such direct deliberations with the Ministry of Justice, the parent ministry for the Immigration Bureau.

NGOs also engage in a third category of action that has no counterpart on local government agendas.[37] These are attempts to change the situation of migrants through domestic and international legal appeals. Domestic legal actions have developed out of the commitment to assist individuals. For example, HELP meets once a month with attorneys affiliated with them to discuss their sponsorship of lawsuits seeking unpaid wages and criminal charges in cases of forced prostitution and physical abuse, and in family law cases involving divorce and child custody. NGOs also sponsor legal action regarding the uncertain citizenship status of children born to migrant women and Japanese men. They see the children of such unions, more than half of whom are illegitimate and thus usually without Japanese nationality, as victims harmed by foreigners' vulnerable position in Japan. Support for individual lawsuits has been provided in hopes of forcing policy change. The goal is to have the Ministry of Justice grant citizenship to such children and visas to their mothers so that they may live in Japan.[38]

---

36. Of course, initial complaints have come from migrants themselves. Until the June 1994 incident involving the spouse of a Japanese citizen, however, migrants alleging abuse had not come to the public's attention. Their accusations, gathered together by NGOs, became even more credible when one young former Immigration Bureau officer stepped forward in December 1994 to report that violent beatings of foreigners in detention was a daily affair (Nyūkan Mondai Chōsakai, *Misshi no jinken shingai*, 126–42). This officer had first reported his horror at these experiences to his high school teachers, two of whom were active in Kalabaw no Kai, a leading support NGO in Yokohama.

37. Likewise, several of the most progressive local governments engage in actions with no counterpart on NGO agendas. Particularly noteworthy are the creation of Foreigners' Advisory Councils by the city of Kawasaki in 1995 and the Tokyo Metropolitan Government in 1997. The councils give foreign residents some voice in local administration, in that they provide a regular forum for local bureaucrats and politicians to meet with foreigners registered in their communities.

38. In fact these efforts have borne some fruit. In July 1996, the Ministry of Justice agreed to allow single foreigners, even if originally illegally in Japan, to receive legal residency on the merits of raising a child with Japanese nationality. This is something the NGOs had aggressively lobbied for, since prior to the administrative turnabout, the foreign parent of a Japanese child was vulnerable to deportation upon being widowed, divorced, or separated. The Ministry of Justice still requires that children of binational parentage be acknowledged by their Japanese parent *prior* to birth in order to receive Japanese nationality for the child and legal residency for the foreign parent—a policy that the NGOs continue to contend.

NGOs' international legal actions take the form of appeals to the United Nations. These should be evaluated as a form of "accountability politics" whereby the NGOs attempt to embarrass the Japanese government into acting to protect migrants in Japan.[39] Although popular opinion in Japan often attributes the problems faced by undocumented migrants to their transgression of the immigration statutes, NGOs use appeals to international fora to reframe the situation in light of governmental responsibilities to protect human rights. These reports uncompromisingly place the blame for exploitation of migrants in Japan on the national government.[40] The Nyūkan Mondai Chōsakai intends to file similar complaints detailing patterns of physical and sexual abuse of foreign migrants while in detention of the Immigration Bureau, and problems that foreigners face in the Japanese justice system in general, including inadequate translation procedures, denial of counsel, failure to inform detainees of their right to remain silent, and excessive periods of detention for violations of the immigration statutes.

THE INSTITUTIONAL POSITION OF NGOS IN JAPAN

Differences in problem definition are one barrier keeping local governments and NGOs from cooperating in their responses to international migration. Another important barrier is the marginalized position of NGOs in Japanese politics.

Public attention to and awareness of Japanese NGOs reached new levels in the mid-1990s.[41] Certainly private organizations that would qualify as examples of citizen participation, or "civil society," have been active in Japan for many years.[42] The recent surge of activity by nongovernmental organizations, although related to "citizens' movements" such as the peace alliances of the 1960s, is sufficiently different to warrant the sense of renewal in alternative political activity. The NGOs support-

---

39. Keck and Sikkink, *Activists beyond Borders*.
40. HELP Asian Women's Shelter, *An Alternative Report (Non-Governmental) to the United Nations* (Tokyo: Mimeograph, 1995).
41. Menju and Aoki ("Japan," 147) report that "according to a keyword search on four major Japanese newspapers, the frequency of articles on NGOs made a jump from 291 during 1991, to 1,032 in 1992, 972 in 1993, and 1,506 in the first ten months of 1994."
42. Margaret A. McKean, *Environmental Protest and Citizen Politics in Japan* (Berkeley: University of California Press, 1981), David E. Apter and Nagayo Sawa, *Against the State: Politics and Social Protest in Japan* (Cambridge: Harvard University Press, 1984), and James W. White, "The Dynamics of Political Opposition," in Andrew Gordon, ed., *Postwar Japan as History* (Berkeley: University of California Press, 1993).

ing foreign migrants are an important component of this new wave of citizen participation.

The entire concept of nongovernmental organizations is legally problematic in the Japanese context. The civil code imposes stringent requirements for the legal incorporation of nonprofit organizations.[43] In order to incorporate, organizations are expected to have operating budgets of ¥30 million backed up by endowments of ¥300 million; to maintain extensive financial records, budgets, and outlines of activities; and to be supervised by a board of "esteemed individuals." Even if all such formal requirements are met, the final decision of whether incorporation will be granted depends upon the discretionary judgment of the national or prefectural ministry responsible for the substantive area of concern.

These requirements have meant that the majority of Japanese NGOs operate without formal status. A 1993 survey conducted by the NGO Promotion Center (NGO Katsudō Suishin Sentaa) determined that 90% of Japanese NGOs active in the international development arena are not legally incorporated.[44] This often limits the scope of their activities by complicating fund-raising and promotional efforts and by precluding the receipt of tax-exempt status. Their operations are further compromised by this situation because, given the inability of NGOs to enter into legal contracts, legal and financial responsibility must be borne by individual members. Nor are Japanese NGOs able to engage easily in arrangements to carry out projects for government or United Nations' agencies.[45]

These institutional barriers to NGO activities in Japan became a topic of political debate in the wake of the Hanshin/Awaji Earthquake of 1995. While the government struggled to organize relief efforts, volunteers from throughout Japan arrived in Kobe and began to provide information, medical care, food, and other necessities to the victims of the quake. Japanese international development NGOs were important leaders in this outpouring of volunteering, contributing their organizational expertise, flexibility, and ability to work in less than ideal circumstances. Critical media coverage of the government inefficacy in the relief effort highlighted the proficiency of NGOs and volunteers of all kinds. Combined with the personal experiences of the volunteers themselves,

---

43. See n.2 above and Menju and Aoki, "Japan."

44. See n. 2 above and Ito, "Tenkanki no NGO katsudō."

45. See n. 2 above; Ito, "Tenkanki no NGO katsudō"; and Thomas Princen and Matthias Finger, "Introduction," in Thomas Princen and Matthias Finger, eds., *Environmental NGOs in World Politics: Linking the Local and the Global* (London: Routledge, 1994).

this coverage prompted a groundswell of interest in how to foster the volunteer ethic in Japanese society.

Government promptly set out to capture the good will toward volunteer NGOs and to channel their activities through formal legal structures. By March 1995, two months after the earthquake, a ministry level commission had been established, bringing together eighteen ministries to study the "volunteer issue." The political parties chimed in as well, looking primarily for ways to provide financial assistance to volunteer organizations.[46]

Ironically, however, this government interest in alleviating the problems associated with their lack of legal status alarmed the NGO community. Many resented what they saw as the one-sided nature of the proposed reforms, and they called upon the government first to encourage a popular debate about the appropriate legal and tax status for the nongovernmental and nonprofit sector in Japan. They were particularly suspicious of the suggestion that new legislation would continue to require all NGOs to receive certification as volunteer organizations at the discretion of government authorities, believing that this type of licensing approach masked a government desire to co-opt the volunteer sector.

The NGO sector has been successful in extending the debate on these proposals and gaining a place for themselves in the negotiations. After being introduced in several previous Diet sessions, the bill Tokutei Hi-eiri Katsudō Sokushin Hō passed in early 1998. It reportedly has the support of many in the NGO community.[47]

PROSPECTS FOR COOPERATION

Although an atmosphere of suspicion between NGOs and local government continues, there is evidence of interest in dispelling it from both sides. Local governments, following the 1995 earthquake, have appreciated the potential for volunteer activity in many different policy areas. Regarding immigration-related issues in particular, those local governments with the most progressive stances of outreach to their foreign residents are increasingly aware that NGOs are able to do things that the governments themselves cannot do. This is especially true regarding undocumented migrants. Even when local governments are willing to

---

46. See n. 2 above and Ito, "Tenkanki no NGO katsudō."

47. A rough translation of this law would be "Designated Law for the Promotion of Nonprofit Activities." See discussion on the reception of the law from the Keidanren (Japanese language website, accessed March 1998).

challenge the exclusionary spirit of national immigration law by creating policies that incorporate foreign residents into the community, they are constrained legally from including undocumented migrants in their efforts. One official from Kawasaki explained to me that the legal constraint is believed appropriate by most local bureaucrats: as officials of the Japanese state, they are disinclined to accept the NGOs' stance that compliance with immigration laws is an irrelevant prerequisite for receiving public services.[48] Yet they appreciate the capacity of NGOs to respond where they cannot. An official in Kawasaki's international office explained to me that there is a progression of ideas for policy-making in this area: first, the NGOs suggest an innovation; second, the local governments begin to implement it; and finally (with any luck), the national government will provide support.

NGOs too see a need for cooperation. Reporting to supporters on discussions at the Third National Forum (1993) of NGOs that support foreign migrants, a member of HLS no Kai wrote the following:

> Local governments are racking their brains to come up with ways to respond to foreign workers, especially in the area of health care policy. [One speaker] noted that although local bureaucrats often claim that they are required to report to national officials, the truth of the matter is there are many sympathetic local officials who could become first contacts in grass-roots initiatives.[49]

In addition to the question of health care policy, NGOs recognize the limits of their capacity to resolve problems facing female migrants involved in the sex industry. Several shelters for such women are run by NGOs, yet the financial burden and need for specialized counseling involved in such enterprises has made this another area where NGOs see the value of cooperation with local government.[50] And in fact the oldest of these shelters, Jōsei no Ie HELP, does receive fairly substantial financial support from the Tokyo Metropolitan Government.

NGOs have also taken note of the local government efforts to include incorporation programs in local internationalization projects. At the 1996 National Forum in Fukuoka, one resolution called for local governments to adopt appropriate international policy frameworks. This

48. Interview, November 1995.
49. HLS no Kai *Newsletter,* no. 36, June 1, 1993.
50. *Kalabaw no Kai,* vol. 25, May 1992, preface.

proposal was singled out as the draft resolution was debated in the closing general session. The activists who had drafted the resolution explained that local governments needed to be encouraged to "internationalize" in a meaningful way and not to succumb to pressures to follow the national government's lead in this policy area. They argued that the NGOs could teach local governments about the various United Nations' agreements prohibiting discrimination against foreign migrants and their families, and that local governments could protect the human rights of migrants even though the national government will not do so.

Some intellectuals involved in discussions of immigration to Japan enthusiastically encourage partnership between NGOs and local government on internationalization issues. In addition to appealing to universal standards of human rights, intellectuals appeal to the new role that the local grass-roots level has in a global age. The slogan "Think Global, Act Local" is a popular refrain and has even been adopted as the name of one group, in Kawasaki, of local bureaucrats and intellectuals who want to help foreign migrants form their own organizations. Intellectuals envision such local grass-roots activity as resting upon a cooperative partnership:

> High expectations for the resolution of global problems affecting international society are being entrusted to the cooperation of local governments and NGOs . . . movement toward their resolution rests in part on international, state-level cooperation, but the cooperation of local government and NGOs at the community level is indispensable.[51]

The purpose of the Tokyo Metropolitan Government seminar, to which these expectations were addressed, was

> to host a seminar for promotion of leadership in internationalization that would address itself to building a new network between officials from the Tokyo Metropolitan Government, Tokyo municipalities, and private leaders of activist international exchange and international cooperation; by coming together to study and discuss the theme of "toward building society in harmony with foreigners."

51. From a speech given by Professor Ebashi Takashi to the Tokyo Metropolitan Government's four-day seminar, "Gaikokujin to Kyōsei suru Shakaizukuri wo Mezashite," held February 6–9, 1996, on local internationalization.

The February 1996 seminar, which lasted four days, brought together almost forty local bureaucrats and forty activists for a series of lectures and small-group discussions on themes such as "Using the media to exchange information," "Thinking about recent issues facing foreign workers," and "Internationalization in our backyards: a social education approach." Discussions were surprisingly blunt and rather heated, with NGO activists in particular willing to point out the shortcomings of local governments. Each day's session ended with informal parties intended to foster personal ties between the bureaucrats and activists.

Similar attempts to bring together local bureaucrats and NGO members hosted by the Kanagawa Social Welfare Council (Kanagawa-ken Shakai Fukushi Kyōgikai) began in 1995. Here too, concerned academics nurtured attempts to foster cooperation through personal exchanges between participants from both groups of local actors. This group met in monthly seminars studying topics such as localized incorporation of immigrants in other advanced industrial democracies. Participants in this roundtable also engaged in heated debates, realistically pointing out the shortcomings of both sides' programs.

CONCLUSION

Cooperation between local government and NGOs in forming a community-based response to international migration to Japan is likely to remain tentative for the short term. Efforts at "local internationalization" are still a marginal part of local government agendas. The NGOs that support foreign migrants continue to struggle for resources. The ties between them remain few and tentative. Nonetheless, the parallel efforts of local governments and NGOs have expanded the boundaries of Japanese debates about immigration. Press coverage of their activities is quite extensive. NGO representatives frequently serve as the primary source of information for newspaper articles on migrants' situations, which introduce the critical perspective on the Japanese treatment of migrants to public discourse. Reports on local government efforts at incorporation programs use their rhetoric to portray increased foreign populations as a positive source of local internationalization. If either group is to succeed in meeting the long-term goals of internationalizing Japanese society to the extent that Japanese can really live in harmony with their new foreign neighbors, then they must persuade the public to endorse these goals as well. Media coverage is a potentially powerful tool toward this end.

The prospects for realizing a peaceful incorporation of foreign migrants would be increased if local governments and NGOs would cooperate on issues where their agendas overlap. In particular, coordination of their individual counseling efforts could increase migrants' access to the formal protections afforded them under Japanese law. Properly enforced, labor regulations and antiprostitution laws, two examples, could go a long way toward solving some of the more egregious cases of exploitation. Perhaps the most promising avenue for working toward a partnership between these actors are the attempts to increase personal ties and lines of communication between NGO activists and the sympathetic bureaucrats working in local international offices. These contacts are still in their early stages and will require all the nurturing like-minded individuals such as academics have to give. In general, however, a great deal of policy innovation occurs in incremental steps, from tentative political experiments like these. Since both sides stand to benefit from a partnership—local government gaining the expertise of NGOs active on the "frontlines," while NGOs gain the superior resources of local government—it seems likely that enough tenacious individuals will continue to build on the nascent ties currently in place, until someday a partnership is achieved in this area.

Looking beyond the limits of the specific debates of immigration politics, these findings demonstrate that small NGOs and local governments deserve more attention than they have generally received in the study of Japanese politics. NGOs are adeptly transforming information gained from their direct experiences into political currency, by casting themselves as a dependable source of fresh information for the mass media. Local bureaucrats are pursuing innovative policies that contradict national priorities, even when they do not have explicit support from local voters or their elected representatives. We neglect these actors from our research at the risk of overlooking the introduction of new ideas and policy priorities onto public agendas.

Challenging National Authority: Okinawa Prefecture and the U.S. Military Bases

Sheila A. Smith

On the evening of November 15, 1998, as television stations announced early returns from cities and towns throughout Okinawa Prefecture, it was clear that the curtain had fallen on one of the most intriguing episodes of political challenge in Japan.[1] Ōta Masahide, the man who had come to represent the voice of Okinawa, had been defeated in the gubernatorial election. Since 1995, when U.S. military personnel were apprehended for the rape of an Okinawan schoolgirl, Okinawa's governor had confronted Japan's national government over its handling of the U.S. bases in Okinawa. Ōta refused to accept Tokyo's directives that he cooperate in base land expropriation procedures, and he put forward a proposal for the withdrawal of U.S. bases from Okinawa by the year 2015.

From 1995 to 1998, the governor explored a variety of avenues to advocate the prefecture's position. He appealed to Japan's court system for a clarification of the Local Autonomy Law; he made annual trips to Washington, D.C. to convince U.S. policymakers and the American public of the need for a change in U.S. basing policy; he supported the organization of a prefectural referendum on the base issue; and he met regularly with citizens' groups working on issues related to the presence of the bases. Finally, Ōta met a total of seventeen times with Prime Minister Hashimoto to attempt to negotiate a way forward on the reduction of U.S. bases in Okinawa. He captured national attention not simply because of his protest against the U.S. military bases, but also because his actions as governor of Okinawa presented a new kind of local politician—one

1. I would like to thank Masaaki Gabe, Ellis Krauss, T.J. Pempel, Patricia Steinhoff, and William J. Tyler for their comments on earlier drafts of this paper. I would also like to thank the Department of Political Science and International Relations of the University of the Ryukyus, the International Institute for Japanese Studies (Kyoto), and the Japan Society for the Promotion of Science for their research support during 1998–99.

that was willing to go up against the power of the national government when its policies undermined local welfare.

In spite of all this national attention, however, Ōta failed to convince Okinawa's voters to continue their support of him. Inamine Keiichi, a challenger who declared he was in the running only three months prior to the election, defeated Ōta by 37,464 votes. Like Ōta, Inamine was not a politician by trade. He was a prominent member of Okinawa's business elite. In contrast to Ōta, he had a quiet personal style, and it was widely rumored that he was a reluctant candidate. In the debates between Inamine and Ōta that preceded the election, Inamine criticized the governor's spending of public money for projects that failed to create jobs or generate income, and he promised Okinawans that he would be able to better negotiate Okinawa's interests with Tokyo. Inamine argued for a prefectural leader who could make things happen rather than someone who espoused ideals without results. Whatever his personal reservations, Inamine's campaign was well organized and energetic, and his sound trucks and posters dominated the streets of central Okinawa once the official campaign period began. In Ginowan City, home to the well-known Futenma Marine Air Station, Inamine campaigners went door to door arguing that a vote for their candidate would mean that at last the base would actually be removed from the community.

The gubernatorial election had been long awaited by Tokyo, and while Liberal Democratic Party (LDP) politicians made a deliberate point of staying away from the island, national political support for Inamine was channeled through other organizations, including national business and medical associations. In contrast, national political leaders from the opposition parties, including Hatoyama Kunio from the Democratic Party and Doi Takako from the Social Democratic Party, came to the island to show their support for Governor Ōta. The Komeitō, one of Ōta's backers in the 1994 election, did not decide on a party position until two weeks before the election. With its local membership split over the base relocation issue, Komeitō finally took the unusual position that, while the party supported Governor Ōta's policies, it would allow its members to vote freely. Perhaps most importantly strains among the progressive prefectural parties had surfaced the previous year when Ōta's vice-governor, Yoshimoto Masanori, failed to be reappointed by the prefectural assembly.[2] After three years of trying to negotiate a compromise on the base

2. Vice-Governor Masanori Yoshimoto was credited with much of the thinking behind the Cosmopolitan City idea and was a major behind-the-scene negotiator for the Okinawa prefectural government in talks with Tokyo officials. His connection to NIRA's

issue with Tokyo, the coalition that had supported the governor was torn between those who thought that no policy short of the removal of U.S. forces was tolerable and those that recognized the need for a phased approach to reducing the U.S. bases.

Ōta's policy on the bases, however, seemed less at issue than his approach to relations with the central government. An *Asahi Shimbun-Okinawa Taimusu* poll taken just prior to the election revealed a strong majority in favor of the base policies that Ōta espoused.[3] But there were clear signs that the chill in relations with Tokyo had many Okinawans worried. For a time, Ōta's confrontation with Tokyo seemed to produce results, including the U.S.-Japan agreement to return Futenma—a conspicuously problematic base located in the densely populated central region of the island. Live-fire exercises on the island were terminated, and new mechanisms for policy consultations between the prefectural and national governments were created. Prime Minister Hashimoto met with the governor, and for a time it seemed as if Ōta would be successful in moving U.S. bases off the island. Moreover, local citizens in Nago City had successfully halted the plan developed in Tokyo to construct a new heliport off of the coast of their community. Yet, when the governor announced on February 7, 1998 that he would reject any further attempt by the national government to relocate U.S. military forces on Okinawa, a chill descended over his relationship with Hashimoto and the bureaucracies charged with finding a solution to Okinawa's problems. Economic development projects designed to ease the burden on local cities, towns,

---

President Shimokobe was thought to have been the main line of communication prior to direct talks with Prime Minister Hashimoto. Yoshimoto was also widely viewed as a pragmatist, who was willing to talk about base consolidation in return for national support for the prefecture's goals. His favorable stance on moving the Naha military port to Urasoe City got him into trouble with the Communist Party, revealing the strains within the progressive coalition that supported Ōta's government. On November 23, 1997, the prefectural assembly vote to reappoint the vice-governor failed to produce the required majority, and Yoshimoto resigned from office. This was the second time that his reappointment was rejected within a predominantly progressive assembly, revealing the depth of divisions within Ōta's *shiji botai*.

3. The poll was conducted by the Asahi Shimbun and the Okinawa Taimusu on November 8-9, 1998. The results were published on November 10, five days before the election. Fifty-one percent of respondents thought that the issue that defined this election was the economy, compared with only 25% that saw the issue as being the bases. When asked specific questions about what policies on the bases were appropriate, however, a majority argued that the U.S. military should be relocated outside of Okinawa Prefecture. A 65% majority also argued that the SACO agreement forged between the U.S. and Japanese governments should be revised to incorporate local opinion.

and villages were halted, and national government support for a long-term plan for restructuring the Okinawa economy evaporated.[4] The ¥5 billion fund specially earmarked by the prime minister for studies on Okinawa's future as a technological and educational center was spent instead on feasibility studies by national government entities, but little new money—hinted at throughout the year long deliberations between Ōta and Hashimoto—was forthcoming from Tokyo. The theme of Okinawa's economic troubles overshadowed all else during the election campaign, and it produced the impression that the prefectural economy would suffer further under Ōta.[5]

Okinawa Prefecture's attempt to change Tokyo's policy on the U.S. bases provides a revealing glimpse at the role of local politicians in articulating citizen protest in Japan. Muramatsu Michio in his study of local influence within Japan has called for greater investigation of the ways in which local governments can influence national policy.[6] His argument that overlapping authority between central and local government provides latitude for local initiative suggests that the greater the "politicization" of local governments, the more advantageous it is to ensuring that local interests are effectively translated into national policy choices. But the Okinawa case suggests that further refinement of Muramatsu's thesis may be in order. As Patricia Maclachlan points out in her chapter on information disclosure efforts at the local level,[7] the success of "politicized" local officials in injecting local interests into the na-

4. On August 19, 1996, the Okinawa Beigun Kichi Shozai Shichōson ni Kansuru Kondankai was formed at the direction of the cabinet secretary to develop policies that would ease the strain on the localities that hosted U.S. bases in Okinawa. This committee was headed by Professor Shimada Haruo of Keio University and came to be known as the Shimada Kon. After surveying the localities in Okinawa, the committee issued a report on November 19 outlining the steps needed to contribute to local development. It also suggested changes in U.S. base policies that affected local residents, changes in the subsidy system, and specific projects for twenty localities. There was a strong emphasis on projects in northern towns and villages, as a result of the heliport initiative.

5. Ōta did not challenge Inamine to produce his own long-term plan for the future of the prefectural economy, and surprisingly, the challenger who came from Okinawa's business elite did not produce his own vision for economic development. He simply said that he was working on it urgently. Despite all the dire predictions about the prefectural economy during the campaign, the Economic Planning Agency in its report on regional economic performance gave Okinawa high marks for its relative vitality. Nonetheless, approximately 80% of prefectural economic activity is linked to national subsidies, distributed either via the Okinawa Development Agency or directly to local governments.

6. Michio Muramatsu, *Local Power in the Japanese State*, translated by Betsey Scheiner and James White (Berkeley: University of California Press, 1997).

7. See "Information Disclosure and the Center-Local Relationship in Japan," above.

tional policy agenda is more likely if citizen activism supports local government initiative. Citizen support for local government efforts to change policy becomes crucial if local interests clash with national policy priorities. Organized citizen protest in Okinawa against the government's policy of sponsoring U.S. military bases there drew national attention and shocked the national government by its intensity. Moreover, alongside citizen efforts to protest the policy, the governor used a variety of measures of citizen opinion, including most notably the prefectural referendum on the bases, to increase his leverage in talks with the national government. It was this potent combination of citizen activism and the advocacy of local interests over national priorities by Okinawa's governor that focused national attention on the impact of the bases.

But the Okinawa case also reveals a more complex interaction: the converging and contradictory demands made upon locally elected officials as a result of their assigned role in national policy administration and, concomitantly, by their obligations to their constituents. Opposing existing national government policies in many cases means challenging the procedures and processes by which policy is made. Local governments are entwined by a complex set of administrative laws that set out the obligations and responsibilities of local officials in the implementation of policy. Indeed, it was this structure that gave Ōta the initial opportunity to contest Tokyo's policy of continuing to offer land for the U.S. military bases. While local politicians have refused to abide by national laws in other instances of social protest in Japan,[8] Ōta played a strikingly visible role in the protest of U.S. bases in Okinawa. Summoned by the citizens who organized the prefectural rally in October 1995, he was in essence given the mantle of leadership of the movement. But Ōta seemed to shift roles over time. He supported citizen efforts to organize the prefectural referendum in 1996 even though many of his critics accused him of lending the power of the prefectural offices to the effort. His ultimate refusal of the new heliport was justified in terms of repre-

8. In contrast to other cases of social protest in postwar Japan, the Okinawa base protest was notable in the sense that a local politician took the leading public role in the expression of challenge against the state. In the citizens' movement organized in protest of pollution, local politicians were not visible players. Nor were local officials very conspicuous in their defense of local interests in the national government's expropriation of farmland to build Narita airport. In both of these cases, local politicians were somewhat ignored or sidestepped in the ultimate confrontation between citizens and the national government. See Margaret McKean, *Environmental Protest and Citizen Politics in Japan* (Berkeley: University of California Press, 1981) and David Apter and Nagayo Sawa, *Against the State: Politics and Social Protest in Japan* (Cambridge: Harvard University Press, 1984).

senting citizen interests as they were revealed in the Nago City referendum in December 1997. But Ōta separated himself from the talks between the Nago City office and the Defense Agency, and from the efforts to organize citizen protest of the heliport initiative. His silence in this final phase of the confrontation between Okinawa and Tokyo ultimately opened him up to criticism from the citizens who wanted him to represent their protest movement, as well as from those local officials who sought his guidance in dealing with the administrative obligations placed upon them by Tokyo.

Once Ōta had compelled Tokyo to pay attention to the protest against the bases, the negotiations for a compromise between national authorities and Okinawan citizens began. But negotiating a reduction of U.S. bases required both the fiscal and regulatory resources of the national government. Ultimately, a compromise between the governor and Tokyo was necessary. In Nago City too, the local mayor was faced with the dilemma of choosing to compromise with Tokyo or representing citizens opposed to the construction of a new base. With opinion split, Mayor Higa accepted Tokyo's proposal but simultaneously resigned as mayor. In the end, Ōta chose to stand with citizen activists and to reject the policy option offered by Tokyo. His electoral defeat reveals similar consequences: on the base issue, it would seem that a viable compromise between the two roles of national policy administrator and citizen advocate has yet to be found.

Moreover, the past three years have made it clear that local interests in Okinawa diverge sharply from national policy priorities. In this case, the avenues for influencing national policy are restricted under the current structure of local-national relations in Japan. It is here that Japan's effort to decentralize government will be tested. The particularities of the Okinawa base protest of 1995–98 offer broader insights into the changing expectations of governance in Japan and also suggest that the needs of localities—however discontent they may be with national policy—will require greater attention in the future. The designation of locally elected officials as agents of the national government is to be removed from the national-local government relationship. In its stead, national government will need to persuade and cajole local officials to implement policy. Local governments too will need to be more active in expressing their needs, and in ensuring that these needs are incorporated into national policy earlier in the policy-making process. This suggests a new relationship between local and national politicians, one that will rely not only on the bargaining skills of local politicians but also on their policy expertise.

This chapter examines the efforts made by Ōta to resolve the Okinawa base crisis from the fall of 1995 to the fall of 1998. Part one examines the linkages between national policy and localities in the administration of U.S. military bases. Part two presents the initial challenge by the prefectural government in the courts concerning the role of the governor in the policy-making process.. Part three presents the terms of the negotiations that unfolded between Okinawa Prefecture and Tokyo over their responses to the base problems. Part four focuses on the way in which Tokyo sought to gain local acceptance for its plan to relocate U.S. forces from the central part of the island to the northern. While Ōta played a central role in the deliberations with Tokyo over how to redress the imbalances in national policy over the bases, he was not the sole actor in this complex case of local challenge to national policy. In his capacity as governor, however, Ōta's actions bring into high relief the contradictions faced by locally elected officials in Okinawa as they attempted to cope with Tokyo's expectations of them as national policy administrators (gyōsei no shuchō) and local citizens' expectations of them as representatives of their community. The Okinawa base protest, however, also makes abundantly clear the limitations faced by local politicians who attempt to sustain a policy of challenge against the national government.

NATIONAL POLICY AND THE U.S. BASES IN OKINAWA

Japanese national policy on the U.S. bases in Okinawa is not one single policy, but several. Therefore, national policy-making processes overlap with local politics only in selected aspects. The maintenance of U.S. bases on Japanese territory is a condition of the U.S.-Japan bilateral security treaty, and as such, it is a component of Japan's foreign and security policies. The U.S.-Japan alliance has been the axis of Japan's postwar foreign policy. Even as the cold war that sponsored the alliance ended, the two governments continued to advocate the importance of the alliance in their overall international relations. As a matter of fact, in 1992, the two governments began to explore ways to reaffirm and redefine the relationship of security cooperation in order to meet the needs of a changing international environment. The presence of U.S. military forces on Japanese territory is deemed central to the implementation of the bilateral security treaty, and Article VI of that treaty stipulates that it is the Japanese government's obligation to provide the U.S. with bases and facilities.

Despite the national political clash between the ruling LDP and progressive political parties over Japan's role in the U.S.-Japan alliance in the 1950s and 1960s, the administration of the U.S. military presence in

Japan has been a quiet affair for Japanese foreign and defense policy-makers for some time now. There have been periodic local complaints over specific incidents and problems associated with the U.S. bases on the main Japanese islands, but by the end of the cold war in 1989, public protest against the U.S. bases seemed to be a thing of the past. For the past decade or more, the defense debate in Japan has focused on Japan's own military role in the alliance and in planning for regional crises in the Asia-Pacific.

As a result, national bureaucrats rather than politicians play the key role in the management of U.S. bases, and they serve as the point of contact between both the U.S. military and local Japanese government officials. The economic and legal division of labor between the U.S. and Japanese governments regarding the administration of U.S. military forces in Japan is outlined in the Status of Forces Agreement (SOFA). Guided by the terms of the SOFA, the Ministry of Foreign Affairs is responsible for managing relations between the local authorities of the host communities and the U.S. Forces Japan (USFJ). Negotiating changes in training schedules, port calls, and considering claims for compensation for accidents, crimes, and other liabilities involving U.S. military personnel are handled through diplomatic channels. Regular consultations between the Japanese government and the U.S. military are held in the U.S.-Japan Joint Military Committee (Nichibei Gōdō Iinkai).

Local governments that have U.S. bases in their jurisdiction have greater interaction with the Japanese Defense Agency, or more specifically, the Defense Facilities Administration Agency (DFAA).[9] The Defense Agency oversees all military bases in Japan, and it is responsible for issues such as the working conditions of Japanese employed on U.S. bases, the provision of goods and services to the bases, and damages incurred by local communities as a result of base operations. Just as there has been a devolution of administrative authority to local governments in other policy areas, local *jichitai* (cities, towns, and villages) have inherited a large amount of related administrative functions associated with the bases. Moreover, this interaction between the Defense Agency and local government has been enhanced since the 1970s as greater subsidies have

---

9. The Defense Facilities Administration Agency maintains offices in Sapporo, Sendai, Tokyo, Yokohama, Osaka, and Naha. The Sapporo office is in charge of all military bases in Hokkaido, which are Japanese Self-Defense Force bases. In contrast, most military bases in Okinawa Prefecture are American, and therefore, the Naha office deals with all of the contentious issues surrounding the maintenance of U.S. bases in Okinawa. The other offices all have administrative responsibilities for several prefecture. The Naha office is the third largest, after the Tokyo and Yokohama offices.

been disbursed to localities that host U.S. military bases. Compensatory funds are provided to offset revenue loss incurred because of the base presence or to build facilities that help shelter local residents from the noise or pollution generated by aircraft, for example. The DFAA also distributes funds that contribute to local development plans. These subsidies provide localities with assistance for building basic infrastructure or facilities needed for providing community services.[10] These latter subsidies are particularly significant in rural or remote localities where other sources of public revenue are relatively scarce. Hence, support within local communities in Japan for U.S. bases has been ensured in large part through financial rewards. Furthermore, as U.S. military forces on Honshu were reduced and consolidated after the Vietnam War, the physical distance of the U.S. military from the densely populated urban centers in Japan ensured that the U.S. military presence remained on the periphery of the public consciousness.

In Okinawa, however, the scale of the U.S. military presence makes it impossible to ignore. The concentration of 75% of all U.S. forces stationed in Japan on the small island is at the root of much of the problem. The bases affect the daily lives of many residents, and local officials must contend with a variety of problems associated with them. As in other regions where U.S. bases are located, the national government has offered Okinawa's localities a broad array of subsidies designed to offset the social costs associated with the base presence.[11] But while the fiscal resources given by Tokyo provide some relief to local communities, the administrative problems associated with the bases are extensive. Of the fifty-three *jichitai* in Okinawa Prefecture, twenty-five contain U.S. military bases and facilities. The sheer density of the bases also extends the impact of their presence to neighboring localities. Noise, pollution, accidents, and crime associated with the military presence are the most obvious complaints, and local governments serve as the first point of contact if there are specific complaints. In some localities, the physical scale

10. In 1974, the Japanese government initiated a system of subsidies specifically designed to provide localities (*jichitai*) with funds for community development. Called the Base Community Improvement Funds (Kichi Shūhen Seibi Shikin), this source of economic assistance to base communities became a major source of local development funding.
11. For some localities, the revenue generated by the bases has been significant. As Naha and the towns and cities in its vicinity have developed, however, the economic benefits of the bases have disappeared, and the costs of maintaining these facilities to the local community far outweigh the benefits. For the more rural communities to the north, the presence of the bases and the revenue they bring in continues to occupy a notable share of local public and private resources.

of the bases has thwarted local attempts at *machi zukuri*, or community planning. In addition, the uneven and unpredictable process of reverting base land to private ownership has meant that localities often
have no option but to plan their towns around the bases.[12] In short, local
governments alone cannot manage the administrative tasks associated
with the U.S. bases, both their maintenance and their conversion to civilian use. The necessary fiscal and regulatory resources can only be
found in Tokyo.

A lesser-known aspect of base policy in Okinawa has been the
need for the DFAA and local governments to implement national land
expropriation regulations. Unlike U.S. bases on Japan's main islands, the
land offered to the U.S. military in Okinawa is expropriated by the state
from private landowners. The legal status of Okinawa's land has long
been the focal point of citizen protest, and the fact that Okinawa was the
only battleground in Japan in the final months of World War II has made
it difficult to resolve individual land claims against the Japanese state.[13]
The forcible expropriation of land by the U.S. military Occupation authorities in the immediate aftermath of the war compounded dissatisfaction over land claims. Indeed, Okinawan landowners organized in the
1950s to claim their property rights against the American authorities.[14]

12. Bases that have been returned to private use, however, have revealed to localities that
the process of managing the transition from base use to civil use is beyond their individual fiscal and administrative capacities. Local government demands for greater national and prefectural assistance in the process of transforming former bases to civilian
use has focused not only on the economic costs and requirements of base conversion.
The legal tangle over ownership and the various regulatory problems inherent in subsequent development projects has also required a new law governing military base conversion (Okinawa ni Okeru Gunyōchi no Henkan ni Tomonau Tokubetsu Sōchihō, or
the Guntenhō). In 1995, the Special Measures Related to the Return of Foreign Base Land
in Okinawa provided for three years of government payments for base land up to a total
amount of ¥1 million. Landowners and local governments alike contend, however, that
this is not sufficient to address the problems associated with transitioning from base
land to civilian use.
13. Several key military facilities on Okinawa were in fact built by the prewar Japanese
military in the final years of World War II. The airfield in Yomitan Village, for example,
was the most significant Japanese military base in the defense of the island, and the
expropriation of land in Yomitan therefore began before the U.S. military expansion
during the Occupation. Today, the question of who owns the land returned in Yomitan
involves claims against the Japanese state that predate the arrival of the U.S. military.
14. For a history of the post-World War II protest movement against U.S. bases by Okinawa
land owners, see, for example, Arasaki Moriteru, *Okinawa—hansen jinushi* (Tokyo:
Kobunken, 1996). For a more personal account written by *hansen jinushi*, see Ahagon
Shōkō, *Inochi koso takara—Okinawa hansen no kokoro* (Tokyo: Iwanami Shinsho, 1992)
and Senda Kakō, Ikehara Hideaki, and Aihara Hiroshi, *Sunao no hansen jinushi* (Tokyo:
Fukinotō Shōbo, 1996).

Furthermore, the use of Okinawa land for military purposes was anathema to many who had suffered through devastating war,[15] and when U.S. bases were used for combat operations in Vietnam, antiwar landowners in Okinawa joined forces with the growing anti-Vietnam War movement.

It was precisely the terms and status of Okinawan bases that were central to negotiations between Tokyo and Washington when the process of reverting Okinawa to Japanese sovereignty began in the late 1960s. The Japanese government's decision to allow the U.S. virtually free reign in the use of the bases after reversion fueled local sentiment that Okinawans were being denied the full protection of the Japanese state and its peace constitution.[16] After Okinawa returned to Japan in 1972, local activism was directed against the Japanese government. It included a broad range of participants: local political parties, labor unions, land owners, local assemblies, and citizens' groups.[17] The national government's treatment of Okinawan landowners, the antiwar sentiments of many Okinawan residents, and the pivotal role played by the bases in the development of local politics, has complicated the national government's relationship with local authorities.

When Governor Ōta confronted Tokyo over its policy toward the U.S. bases in Okinawa in 1995, therefore, there was a deep basis for citizen dissatisfaction. The rape of a twelve-year-old schoolgirl stimulated a broad protest against the way Okinawan interests had been ignored in

15. This forcible expropriation of land, and the relocation of many Okinawa residents during the early years of the U.S. military occupation and through the Korean War, denied Okinawa's land owners access to their land and forced many to live outside of the communities where they were born. Attempts by U.S. Occupation authorities to compensate Okinawa's landowners at marginal prices provoked the first "islandwide protest" (*shimagurumi tōsō*) in the 1950s. Since then, land owner interests were effectively organized in the Tochirenkai, an organization that continues today to represent the 28,000 or so Okinawans who own base land (*gunyōchi*). See *Tochiren 30-nen no ayumi*, 3 vols. (Urasoe, Okinawa: Ushio Insatsu, 1984).

16. Former Prime Minister Sato Eisaku promised that Okinawa would be returned to japan with the same conditions imposed on U.S. bases as were imposed on U.S. bases in Honshu. This promise to consider Okinawa on equal terms (*hondō nami*) with the rest of Japan was broken by Sato in a secret agreement with President Nixon that gave the U.S. the right to introduce nuclear weapons to Okinawa in case of an "emergency." Tokyo's commitment to the same treatment for Okinawa as for other parts of Japan was also seen as suspect when plans to consolidate and reduce U.S. military bases there were implemented only partially in contrast to the conspicuous reduction of U.S. bases in the Kanto region in the late 1970s. For more on the Sato-Nixon agreement, see Wakaizumi Kei, *Tasaku nakarishi wo shinzemuto hossu* (Tokyo: Bungeishunju, 1994

17. For a recent overview of the postwar history of Okinawa, see the commemorative volume prepared by the Okinawa prefectural government based on U.S. and Japanese archival materials, Okinawa-ken Chiji Kōshitsu Kōhōka, ed., *Okinawa—sengo 50-nen no ayumi* (Naha: Naha Shuppansha, 1995).

Tokyo's policy toward the U.S. bases. Tokyo's hesitant response only exacerbated local outrage. The base issue had long been central to Okinawan politics, and Ōta's response to the widespread public dissatisfaction with the national government had a strong base of institutionalized support within the prefecture—most conspicuously among groups associated with the policies of Japan's progressive national political parties. But partisanship explains only part of the reason for the governor's stance. To contend with the problems faced by Okinawa as a result of the bases, the prefectural government needed to recast the domestic compact between national bureaucrats and local *jichitai* leaders that sustained the U.S. military presence in Okinawa.

THE LAW, NATIONAL POLICY, AND LOCAL POLITICIANS

The cooperation of local politicians has been critical to the maintenance of U.S. military bases, and Governor Ōta's refusal to play the role assigned to him in the implementation of land expropriation procedures revealed the nature of the responsibility imposed upon local leaders in maintaining U.S. bases in Okinawa. In particular, the rape and the public outrage it inspired in the fall of 1995 produced a political crisis, not only for Tokyo but also for Okinawa's local politicians. Bureaucrats in Tokyo responded slowly to public outrage in Okinawa. Initial meetings between Governor Ōta and the Minister of Foreign Affairs produced little demonstrable action on behalf of Okinawa, and this seeming indifference in Tokyo only fueled public dissatisfaction within the prefecture. The prefectural assembly and mayors of the cities, towns, and villages of Okinawa issued resolutions of protest against the existing SOFA,[18] yet it was the widespread citizen protest that reverberated across Japan. The SOFA and its implementation were of concern to a number of other localities in Japan,[19] and in the face of Tokyo's indifference, Okinawan political leaders found common cause with other municipal mayors, prefectural governors, and citizens' groups who also faced the presence of foreign mili-

18. By September 23, 1995, fifty of the fifty-three *jichitai* in Okinawa had already passed or were planning to pass Resolutions of Protest against the rape. *Ryūkyū Shimpō*, September 23, 1995.

19. For an example of how another prefectural government has viewed the impact of the SOFA on its residents and on its ability to govern, see Kanagawa-ken, Hōgaibu Kichitaisakuka, ed., *Zainichi beigun chii kyōtei gairon: chihō jichitai tono kanrende* (Kanagawa: Hakuensha, 1993). For a more critical perspective on how the base presence infringes on the rights of Japanese citizens, see Yokohama Benoshikai, ed. *Kichi to jinken* (Tokyo: Nihon Hyōronsha, 1989).

tary in their communities.[20] In the face of growing public criticism, the Foreign Ministry began consultations with the U.S. government on how to respond to the call for greater Japanese jurisdiction over suspected offenders.[21]

But, more significantly, it was Ōta's decision to reject the role assigned to him in the legal procedures for expropriating Okinawan land for the U.S. military that transformed public protest into political crisis and pitted the prefectural government against Tokyo. When Okinawa reverted to Japanese sovereignty in 1972, approximately 2,000 Okinawan landowners refused to enter into contracts with Tokyo. They organized themselves into a loose coalition of *hansen jinushi* (or antiwar landowners). It is the land owned by the *hansen jinushi*, therefore, that has been expropriated by the state, and the legality of this expropriation has plagued the national government's policy on U.S. bases in Okinawa ever since.

A number of provisional laws have been drafted since 1972 to assert national government control over base land (*gunyōchi*) in Okinawa. Initially, the DFAA drafted a law that provided for the "provisional use" of land in Okinawa, claiming control over base land for five years.[22] When this law was due to expire in 1977, the DFAA drafted a new law that would have renewed national control for the next decade. But opposition in the Diet forced the law to be rescinded. Instead a newly revised law was adopted to claim control over the land until the process of clarifying prop-

20. Statements of protest were issued by localities around Japan. For the most part, the requested revisions focused on Japan's right to prosecute criminals (Article 17) and on putting an end to the separate system of justice for U.S. military personnel and their dependents stationed in Japan. Moreover, the Hōgai Kankei Shuyō Tōdōfūken Chiji Renryaku Kyōgikai (or Hōgai Chijikai), an organization comprised of governors around the country who had bases in their region, began to consult on a joint resolution against the SOFA and to call for its revision. On October 13, after a meeting attended by fourteen Hōgai Chijikai governors in Tokyo, a joint resolution was passed calling for steps to prevent a recurrence of the rape incident and for a revision of Article 17 of SOFA.
21. By the following spring, the U.S. and Japanese governments decided to revise the manner in which they implemented the prosecution of criminals under SOFA. In cases of severe crimes, including murder and rape, suspects would be handed over to Japanese authorities prior to indictment if both U.S. military and Japanese prosecutors agreed on the evidence. The first case where this new "interpretation" of SOFA was applied was in an incident on the main islands (Sasebo City) where a U.S. military serviceman attacked a Japanese woman with a knife in the summer of 1996. Two more criminal cases involving U.S. Marine personnel occurred in the fall of 1998. Both were cases of drunk driving, and in one, a high school student was killed. Neither of these incidents, however, was considered severe enough by the Japanese government to warrant transfer of the alleged criminal into Japanese custody prior to indictment.
22. This law was called the Law Related to the Provisional Use of Public Land in Okinawa (Okinawa ni Okeru Kōyōchi Nado no Kantei Shiyō ni kan suru Hōritsu).

erty rights and boundaries was complete.[23] Moreover, in 1982, the Japanese government resuscitated an old law that had been used in the early postwar years with regard to U.S. military bases on the main islands, and applied it to Okinawa. The law asserted the right of the central government to exert control over land as a result of its obligations in the U.S.-Japan security treaty to provide the U.S. with military bases. Henceforth, government control over the land was based on the domestic law that allows the state to expropriate private land.[24]

Since 1982, therefore, the land for U.S. bases has been expropriated by Tokyo under the provisions set forth under the Land Expropriation Law (Tochi Shūyōhō), which sets forth the basis for state expropriation of private land for public purposes.[25] It is important to note, however, that Japan's Land Expropriation Law does not stipulate the state's right to expropriate land for military purposes. Therefore, the patchwork of "special measures" established for the Okinawa bases sidesteps an important legal restriction on the activities of the postwar Japanese state. The roundabout legal maneuvering undertaken to cope with the issue of Okinawa bases has provided the basis for the national government to claim that its policy is procedurally in keeping with the intent of the Constitution. Yet it has exacerbated the perception within Okinawa that the national government has less regard for the rights of Okinawans than other Japanese citizens.[26]

23. As a result of the legislative battle, the national government's legal claim on the land lapsed, and for four days, many antiwar landowners entered the bases to demonstrate their legal right to occupy the land. At the time, there were still 500 landowners that refused to sign contracts with the Defense Agency. One *hansen jinushi*, Shimabukuro Zenyū, took his family and his tractor to his land to plant garlic. Others went to their land, then a Japanese Self-Defense Force Base, each day for a picnic. Another well-known antiwar landowner, Ahagon Shōkō, took forty to fifty of his friends to his land to plant trees. This four-day interval is referred to as the "four days when the wind blew through the U.S.-Japan security treaty" (*anpōni kazeana o aketa yokkakan*).

24. By 1982, the number of *hansen jinushi* was dwindling. When the new law was passed, a political campaign to reinforce the strength of the *hansen jinushi* organized the sale of small parcels of land by supporters within and without the prefecture. These supporters, called *hitotsubo hansen jinushi* (or one-*tsubo* antiwar landowners) expanded the number of the antiwar landowners to about 2,000 again.

25. Local voice in the land expropriation process is exercised through the Land Expropriation Council, which is bound to hold public hearings and make a judgment on the validity of the government's claim to the land. The DFAA represents the national government during this process and handles the disbursement of rent and other procedural requirements related to landowner claims against the state.

26. For a contemporary analysis of how the Japanese government has ignored the postwar constitution in its policy toward the U.S. bases in Okinawa, see Takara Tetsumi, *Okinawa kara mita heiwa kenpō—umanchū ga shūyaku* (Tokyo: Miraisha, 1997).

Local officials, as agents of national authority, have been required to take part in the Land Expropriation Laws procedures.[27] Local officials are obliged to act as proxies for landowners at two steps in the implementation procedures.[28] The first is when the DFAA seeks to gain the consent of the landowner to use the land. If a landowner refuses, then the local mayor is asked to sign in his/her stead (*shomei daikō*). At a later stage in the procedure, the government must obtain confirmation that the land it seeks to expropriate is indeed the same land as the landowner recognizes as his/her land (*kōkoku jūran*). Again, if a landowner refuses to participate in the process, then the local mayor is asked to provide this confirmation in the landowner's stead. In both cases, if the mayor refuses to sign the documents, then the governor of the prefecture is called upon to sign for the landowners. Three local mayors in Yomitan Village, Okinawa City, and Naha City had refused to sign as proxies for protesting landowners, but until 1995, no governor had ever refused the obligation to do so. Even Governor Ōta had signed leases during his first term in office, despite a campaign promise to refuse to cooperate.

Frustrated with Tokyo's lack of attention to the public protest over the rape, and the lack of prefectural influence over base policy, Ōta saw the land expropriation procedures as an opportunity to gain national attention to Okinawa's plight. His refusal to sign impending leases, which were to expire the following spring, interrupted the procedural requirements that maintained the legal basis of the Japanese government's control over contested land.[29] On September 28, the governor announced in the prefectural assembly that, in view of his concerns about the efforts of the U.S. and Japanese governments to reinforce and expand their se-

27. The role of local government as an agent of national authority is clearly stipulated in the Land Expropriation Law's procedures, and like other administrative laws in Japan, these procedures reflect the established hierarchy of agency among local, prefectural, and central authorities. If a governor refuses to sign the leases on behalf of those land owners who refused contracts, they are subject to an order by the cabinet minister responsible (in this case the director general of the DFAA and/or an order by the prime minister). If the governor fails to respond to this directive from the central government, then it is up to the courts to determine whether or not the governor must comply with national policy in his/her capacity as an agent of the central government.

28. For an full explanation of this process, see Nakachi Hiroshi, "Gunyōchi kyōsei shiyō shokumu shikkō meirei sōshōni," *Hōritsu jihō* 68.4 (April 1996): 17-22.

29. During his first term in office, Governor Ōta and his prefectural government faced a number of base-related policy issues that he had inherited from his conservative predecessor, Governor Nishime, who had governed Okinawa during the 1980s. In 1991, Ōta complied with procedures and signed leases on behalf of these landowners (*dairi shomei*) despite arguments by his supporters that he should refuse.

curity collaboration, he had decided it was in the best interests of the prefecture for him to refuse to participate in the process of government expropriation of private land. This was the first time in Okinawa's postreversion history that a governor had represented the antiwar landowners and their claims against the state. More importantly, he had broad support within the prefecture for this action, and in subsequent opinion polls, he was praised for having given a voice to Okinawan interests.

Tokyo's initial response was to negotiate with the governor in an attempt to avoid a public confrontation. After Ōta announced his refusal to sign for the landowners, the director general of the DFAA, Hōshuyama Noboru, visited Okinawa to discuss the issue with the governor. Hōshuyama stated at a press conference that the government had no intention of initiating legal proceedings against the governor—which would be the next step in the process of gaining access to the land. He said that Tokyo wished to discuss the issue with the governor in a "sympathetic" spirit. Ōta refused to meet the director general, and Hōshuyama returned to Tokyo after several days of waiting in Naha. Ōta's refusal was a public rejection of national authority, and it received widespread press coverage throughout Japan.[30] The following week, Ōta sent his vice-governor, Yoshimoto Masanori, to Tokyo to explain that he intended to "continue the fight in the courts." Ironically, the prime minister at the time, Murayama Tomiichi, was a member of the Social Democratic Party (formerly the Japan Socialist Party). His own political party had been a long-time supporter of the *hansen jinushi* movement prior to its coalition with the LDP.

Meanwhile, throughout Okinawa, local governments and assemblies, and a broad array of prefecturewide associations and citizens' groups, began to organize a mass demonstration.[31] On October 21, 1995, approximately 85,000 Okinawans gathered in a prefectural rally to call for the withdrawal of U.S. military forces and revision of the SOFA. The demonstration was both an Okinawan statement and a citizens' statement. Indeed, the organizers of the Okinawa Prefectural Citizens' Rally (Okinawa Kenmin Sōkekki Taikai) excluded national and local political party leadership from the program. In reviving the memory of the

---

30. Several weeks later, Director General Hōshuyama was again in the headlines for ostensibly saying that the prime minister "was not terribly bright" (*atama ga warui*) since he had not initiated legal proceedings against the governor. Hōshuyama resigned shortly thereafter amid criticism of overstepping his authority as a member of the cabinet and undermining the political control of the prime minister.

31. For full coverage of the events leading up to and following the Okinawa Prefectural Citizens' Rally, see *Kichi Okinawa: igi mōshitate*, vol. 1 (Naha: Ryūkyū Shinpōsha, 1995) and Okinawa Taimusu, ed., *50-nenme no gekido: Okinawa—beigun kichi mondai* (Naha: Okinawa Taimususha, 1996), chapter 1.

"islandwide protest" against the bases of the 1950s, the rally was an especially powerful message to national political leaders of all parties that Okinawans were weary of the way in which they had been ignored by Tokyo. Only one politician played a central role, and he was Okinawa's governor. Ōta addressed the rally and made a public apology to the people of Okinawa for his inability to protect the young victim of the rape and to ensure the welfare of Okinawa's citizens.

The governor's decision to refuse to sign the base leases and the mass demonstration of protest against the Okinawa bases strengthened the prefecture's hand vis-à-vis the central government. On November 4, 1995, almost two months after the rape incident occurred, Ōta finally met with the prime minister. In this meeting, Ōta stated that the prefecture could no longer tolerate the "fifty-year-old burden" of U.S. military bases imposed upon it by Tokyo, and he reiterated that he would not rescind his refusal to sign the leases on behalf of the central government. The governor presented Prime Minister Murayama with a list of revisions that the prefecture wished to see in the SOFA.[32] The prime minister responded by acknowledging that Tokyo had not responded adequately to demands from Okinawa for change, and Murayama expressed his sympathy with the plight of Okinawans. He also agreed to establish a consultative mechanism between the central government and the prefecture concerning the bases—a proposal that the prefectural government had been making to Tokyo for some time. At Ōta's request, this mechanism was placed under the guidance of the prime minister's office so that policy on the Okinawa bases would not reside solely in the hands of the national bureaucrats.[33]

---

32. The amendments of SOFA requested by the Okinawa prefectural government covered an array of issues that had troubled local governments, including the following: clarification of the status of bases and facilities to be returned to civilian use (Article 2); the need for a domestic law governing noise reduction measures (Article 3); clarification and definition of the meaning of "movement" of forces (Article 5); the transfer of base management (Article 6); the provision of Japanese license numbers for U.S. military vehicles (Article 10); the payment of taxes on privately owned vehicles (Article 13); the right of detention of criminal suspects by Japanese authorities (Article 17); and provision of compensation for accidents whether committed on duty or not (Article 18). *Okinawa kara—beigun kichi mondai dokyūmento* (Tolyo: Asahi Shimbunsha, 1997), 69–70.

33. The Committee on U.S. Bases in Okinawa was formally established by cabinet decision on November 17, 1995. Headed by the cabinet secretary, the main members were the prefectural governor, the Minister of Foreign Affairs, and the director-general of the Defense Agency. A working group was formed under this committee, which included the vice-cabinet secretary, the director general of the North American Affairs Bureau (MOFA), the director general of the DFAA, and the vice-governor and the Director of Policy Affairs of Okinawa Prefecture.

But the question of what to do about the leases was a pressing one for Tokyo. Extension of the leases, due to expire at the end of March 1996, needed to be moved forward if the legal basis for the Japanese government's control of the land was to be maintained.[34] On November 21, the prime minister announced his decision to implement Local Autonomy Law procedures. He first advised (*kankoku*) and then ordered (*meirei*) the governor to sign the leases.[35] Ōta met with the prime minister again on the 24th, but there was no change in either position. On December 7, in accordance with procedures set out in Article 151(2) of the Local Autonomy Law, the prime minister asked the Fukuoka High Court (Naha Branch) to order the governor to fulfill his governmental obligation to implement national policy. Thus, Tokyo abandoned its effort to negotiate, and Ōta got his hearing in Japan's courts.[36]

To contend with a policy-making process that had little room for local voice or initiative, the governor of Okinawa, backed by broad public support within his prefecture, sought to move outside the legal structure of his relationship with the central government. Ōta's challenge in the courts went well beyond a technical procedural interpretation of the Land Expropriation Law as it was applied to the U.S. military bases in Okinawa. In both of the two court hearings held in the High Court and the Supreme Court on Ōta's refusal to act as proxy for Okinawan landowners, the prefectural legal team questioned the role assigned to local politicians in the implementation of Tokyo's policies. The prefecture's lawyers contested the basis of determining national authority and argued that the governor's obligation was not to Tokyo but to those who elected him. In short, the Okinawa position went to the heart of the debate over just how much policy-making autonomy was to be given to localities in Japan. In marked contrast, the national government's legal team focused on the administrative procedures to be followed, and therefore, it

---

34. Over the long run, it was the prospect of the leases due to expire the following year that weighed more heavily on the minds of the Defense Agency officials responsible for land expropriation. Three thousand landowners, many of them *hitotsubo hansen jinushi*, would be able to enter on to base land in 1997 when their leases expired. Many of these leases were for land occupied by Kadena Air Force Base and Futenma Marine Air Station, the two largest and most active U.S. military bases on Okinawa.

35. This procedure for enforcing governors to act as agents of the central government "in cases where lack of action by the governor to implement policies related to the authority of the national government creates clear and significant damage to the public interest" is set out in Article 151(2) of the Local Autonomy Law (Chihō Jichihō). (author's translation)

36. The court date was set for December 22, and hearings were held through March 1996.

did not acknowledge the underlying political issue of whether or not the national government could exert authority over a publicly elected official. The provisions set forth under the Land Expropriation Council called explicitly for the governor to act in his capacity as the head of prefectural government to implement national law. As expected, the prefectural legal team called on the court to consider whether the action required by the Land Expropriation Law was constitutional because it involved violating the right to private property. In addition, the prefecture's lawyers argued that implementation of the Land Expropriation Law was not in consonance with the Local Autonomy Law's intent regarding the functions delegated to local authorities by the central government. The prefectural lawyers argued that the prime minister's use of the provisions of the Local Autonomy Law to make the governor to cooperate in the forcible expropriation of land was debatable.[37]

The court hearings also afforded the opportunity to contend that interests of the prefecture's citizens should be the priority for the governor. Ōta himself appeared before the court on March 11 in response to the judge's request that he explain his reasons for refusing to act as proxy for the landowners. The governor was surrounded by *hansen jinushi* in the courtroom, and 500 more supporters gathered outside. In response to the judge's question, the governor argued that since Okinawa's future was at stake, refusing to sign the leases was both in the national (*kokueki*) and in the public (*kōeki*) interest. On March 25, the Fukuoka High Court rendered its judgment that there was no clear evidence that the 1982 Special Measures Law was unconstitutional. Moreover, the judge found that the procedures for land expropriation were "basically rational" (*ichiyō no gōrisei ga mitomerareru*) and, therefore, not illegal. Regarding the prefecture's argument that the governor should not be forced to comply with a procedure that violated the wishes of his constituents, he further argued that the provision of bases to the U.S. was a duty required by

---

37. The prefectural legal team raised two aspects of the national government's suit. The first questioned the applicability of using the Local Autonomy Law's provisions for legal action. According to Article 151, the prime minister can ask the court to order a local official to carry out national policy procedures if the action of the local official "is a clear and egregious violation of the public interest" (*kōeki*). The second aspect focused on the difference between the obligations of a locally elected official to implement centrally delegated tasks as an agent of the central government (*kikan shokkumu*) and the responsibilities of that official as a representative of his community (*jien dantai*). For a discussion of this argument put forward by Okinawa prefectural lawyers, see Nakachi Hiroshi, "Gunyōchi kyōsei shiyō shokumu shikkō meirei sōshōni," and "Chihō jichihō—17-nenburi no daikaisei," *Hō to minshushugi* 259 (July 1997): 58–59.

Japan's obligations (*rikō gimu*) under the U.S.-Japan security treaty. Seen in this light, the judge argued, the governor's actions were clearly in violation of "the public interest" (*kōeki*). In short, the court ruled in favor of the national government's definition of the public interest, as opposed to Ōta's advocacy of the interests of the Okinawan public. It ordered the governor to comply with his duties as the administrative head (*gyōsei no shuchō*) of the prefecture. Two days later, Ōta announced his refusal to obey the court order and his intention to appeal the Fukuoka High Court's decision to Japan's Supreme Court.

Ōta's court challenge of the land expropriation procedures created an urgent, and unprecedented, problem for the DFAA. Under the provisions of the Land Expropriation Law, the prime minister was empowered to go ahead and sign the leases, which he did on March 28, 1996, on the day after Ōta announced his refusal to comply with the High Court's order. But this delayed the procedures required to retain legal government control over the land, and the DFAA confronted the possibility that landowners would claim access to their land when the leases expired on March 31.[38] The most critical lease was for the Sobe Communications Site in Yomitan Village, where part of the land was owned by noted activist and antiwar landowner, Chibana Shōichi.[39] On March 29, the DFAA requested that the Land Expropriation Council grant the government "emergency use" rights for the Sobe site.[40] Yet, with only two days remaining before the leases expired, "illegal occupation" of private land by the state was a foregone conclusion. The Land Expropriation Council set hearings for April 12, arguing that it needed to visit the site and prepare for public hearings. The DFAA announced that the U.S.-Japan security treaty required continued use of the base land. Therefore, base land would continue to be managed by the U.S. military, and Chibana would not be given access to his land. On the morning of April 1, Chibana appeared at the base gate demanding access. During the night, however, the police had erected a fence around the communications site

38. This was the fourth time since Okinawa was returned to Japan that the prefectural Land Expropriation Council had deliberated on the status of the land used for U.S. military bases. It was the first time that a prime minister had signed the leases on behalf of the landlords.

39. For Chibana's own account of his political activism, *see Yakisuterareta hinomaru—kichi no shima Yomitan kara* (Tokyo: Shakai Hikyōsha, 1996).

40. Under the Land Expropriation Law, there is a provision that allows for temporary use by the government of private property if necessary to provide for public safety. This provision is typically applied in cases of natural disasters. This request by the DFAA for such permission was the first time this had been applied to base land in Okinawa.

and had heightened security. As a result, Chibana and his friends stood outside of the gate facing police in full riot gear inside the fence.[41] Okinawa's political protest of the U.S. bases became gripping news on national television.

The land lease battle had been lost locally, but the argument carried forward to the Japanese Supreme Court by Governor Ōta had broader resonance throughout Japan. His appearance before the full court on July 10, 1998 lasted only fifteen minutes, yet it remains, perhaps, his most effective and compelling public statement of Okinawan interests.[42] He began with a brief overview of Okinawa's history, including its colonization by Japan. He pointed out that in contrast to "the military culture" of the Japanese, Okinawans are a pacifist people. He argued that the forcible land expropriation by the U.S. military and the continued maintenance of major U.S. bases on the island after Okinawa's reversion to Japanese control had adversely impacted the social welfare of the Okinawa people. Why was it that Okinawa, and Okinawa alone, he asked, was required to bear the excessive burden of the U.S. bases. The legal question placed before the court by Ōta and his legal team was whether a prefectural governor, as a publicly elected official, was bound to follow a national policy (in this case, the extension of national authority over the land for the bases) that impinged upon the rights of local citizens to a "peaceful life." In contrast to the procedural argument put forward by the national government regarding the obligation of local authorities to implement national bureaucratic prerogatives, Ōta presented the court with the simple political question of who was to represent the citizens of Okinawa.

---

41. Much to the surprise of Defense Agency officials, the Land Expropriation Council turned down their request for "emergency use" of the Sobe Communications Site on May 11, 1996. Stating that the government had not sufficiently stated its need to retain control over the land, nor had it clearly elucidated what exactly the base functions were that were so critical, the council requested that the procedures begin again. Since the director general of the DFAA had been transferred, the council asked that the DFAA correct and resubmit its case. This outcome revealed that the government's influence over the Land Expropriation Council was not what it had assumed. It also suggested to many in the LDP and in the Defense Agency that the law governing the use of land for the U.S. bases in Okinawa needed to be revised before the next group of leases expired in the spring of 1997. Unlike the case of the Sobe site, the leases due for extension in 1997 involved 3,000 land owners who owned parcels of land on Kadena Air Force Base and Futenma Marine Air Station, the two most important bases on the island. On May 14, Chibana Shōichi and his family and friends entered the base and spent several hours on his land playing the *sanshin* and dancing Okinawan folk dances.

42. For the full text of the governor's statement in the Supreme Court, see Ōta Masahide and Okinawa-ken Kichitaisakushitsu, *Dairi shomei kyohi no riyu* (Tokyo: Hitonaru Shobō, 1997).

The Supreme Court rejected the governor's appeal on August 29,[43] ruling that the 1982 Special Measures Law used to expropriate base land was constitutional. This decision represented the end of the legal challenge posed by the prefectural government with regard to the land expropriation practices of the central government. The appeal to the courts to clarify the role of local government in implementing national policy was an attempt by the Okinawa prefectural government to demonstrate the contradictions inherent in the relationship between local and national governments. While ultimately the Japanese Supreme Court rejected this argument, Ōta's testimony raised important questions about the plight of local government in Japan. It was a deft political statement, albeit not a successful legal challenge to Tokyo's authority.[44]

The administrative loophole used by Ōta to register protest against Tokyo's handling of the bases was closed the following spring. The Defense Agency drafted legislation that would revise the process for expropriating Okinawa base lands, and it passed the Diet by a broad majority. In the new 1997 Special Measures Law, contested land is placed under the control of Japan's Ministry of Construction if leases expire until the Land Expropriation Law procedures are completed. This bridging mechanism prevents *hansen jinushi* from demanding access to their land. Accordingly, it prevents the opportunity for legal claims against the state. In effect, the provision circumvents the authority of the prefectural Land Expropriation Council, since it renders any judgment by the committee on DFAA land claims subject to higher review by the national government. The 1997 Special Measures Law neutralized the political clout of the *hansen jinushi* movement, and it removed the opportunity for a governor or other local politicians in Okinawa to interfere with Tokyo's offer of privately owned land to the U.S. military.

BARGAINING WITH THE CENTER

Ōta's legal challenge—as well as the national government's efforts to close the administrative loophole in the procedures for expropriation of base

---

43. The court announced its judgment on August 28, 1996. Judge Miyoshi rejected Governor Ōta's appeal and upheld the first ruling of the High Court in the national government's favor. He argued that if the leases were not signed it would create an obstacle for the fulfillment of the Japanese government's obligations under the U.S.-Japan security treaty. Consequently, the governor's refusal to sign the leases was clearly a striking trespass of the public interest (*kōeki*).

44. It was an unprecedented case in Japan's postwar politics, however, since it was the first time that the national government had appealed to the courts to force a prefectural governor to implement its policy. See Nakachi, "Gunyōchi kyōsei shiyō shokumu shikkō meirei sōshōni."

land—was part of a larger effort to change the balance of bargaining power between Okinawa Prefecture and the national government. Citizen protest in the fall of 1995 prompted the prefectural and national governments to reassess policy on the U.S. bases in Okinawa. Okinawa's governor wanted to assert a greater voice for local government in the policy-making process. Japan's prime minister—by January 1997—needed to demonstrate to the U.S. that there was still sufficient local support for the U.S. military presence. Both Ōta and Hashimoto needed to find a mutually acceptable solution to their confrontation over the bases, and by the summer of 1996 both sides were preparing to resolve the crisis. Garnering political resources was Ōta's first priority. Hashimoto, meanwhile, concentrated on demonstrating that he had Okinawan interests at heart.

The prefectural goal was not only to change Tokyo's policy but also to renegotiate the policy-making process itself by giving the prefectural government a greater role. Because base policy had been primarily in the hands of national bureaucrats and local officials, there was little room in existing policy channels for insertion of the prefectural voice. The lack of sufficient consultation mechanisms and the structure of the base subsidy program made it virtually impossible for Okinawa prefecture to exert influence over base policy. Moreover, the Ōta administration brought a new approach to thinking about the prefecture's future. Under the direction of Ōta and Vice-Governor Yoshimoto, the prefectural government had adopted a new, long-term vision for the future development of Okinawa, called the Cosmopolitan City Formation Concept (Kokusai Toshi Keisei Kōzō). Arguing that past efforts to implement economic development plans for Okinawa had been unsuccessful because of the presence of the bases, the prefecture had commissioned a study that would consider development possibilities in the absence of the bases.[45] This "grand design" for restructuring Okinawa's economy called for the creation of a free-trade zone in Okinawa, and this novel idea became the basis of the prefecture's negotiations with the national government. Instead of returning land to Okinawans base-by-base, the prefectural government advocated a comprehensive and phased reduction of bases on the island, and drafted a Base Return Action Program outlining

---

45. Local support for the prefecture's new vision had yet to be confirmed, however. On January 9, 1996, the prefecture began consultations on the implementation of the Cosmopolitan City Formation Concept with local government leaders. The Shichōson Renryakukai was designed to build local support for the Cosmopolitan City plan and to ensure that the prefecture would speak with a single voice as it proceeded to develop this plan in negotiations with Tokyo.

the steps by which they wanted bases to be closed.[46] In order to implement the Cosmopolitan City Formation Concept, the Base Return Action Program called for complete withdrawal of U.S. forces from Okinawa by the year 2015. This long-term approach to base reduction formed the basis of Governor Ōta's deliberations with Tokyo. On January 30, 1996, at the third meeting of the Consultative Committee on Okinawa Base Problems, the prefecture presented Tokyo officials with their new prefectural vision for the future.[47]

The policy agenda for Tokyo was, of course, the maintenance of the U.S. military presence in Okinawa, and the Okinawa governor's actions on the leases had created an embarrassing crisis for Japan's political leaders. Frustration was mounting within the bureaucracy and the LDP as the "Okinawa base problem" (*Okinawa kichi mondai*) grew, and the ruling coalition (the LDP, the new Sakigake Party, and the Social Democratic Party) renegotiated their compact.[48] Murayama resigned on January 6 amid widespread criticism, and LDP member Hashimoto Ryūtarō formed a new cabinet on January 11, 1996. These changes in Tokyo signaled a determination to attend to the Okinawa base problem, and the anticipated summit meeting between Japan's new prime minister and President Clinton focused Tokyo's attention on finding a way to ensure the future stability of the U.S. military bases.

Meanwhile, bureaucrats responsible for the U.S.-Japan alliance dialogue had already begun to work on a response to the Okinawan protest. On November 20, 1995, the Special Action Committee on Okinawa (SACO) began a review of the status of the bases and the requirements of the U.S. military in order to facilitate the reduction and consolidation of

46. The Base Return Action Program outlined a three-stage program of base closure. In the first stage (1996–2001), the aim was to focus on bases already requested for return in time for the end of the Third Okinawa Promotion and Development Plan. The second phase (2002–10) was to meet the term of the National Comprehensive Development Plan. The final stage would culminate the process in 2015. See Okinawa Prefectural Government, *Base Return Action Program (proposal)*, January 1996 (English version).
47. Prime Minister Murayama created this committee in December, and the previous meeting had focused on noise abatement measures required by communities next to Kadena Air Force Base and Futenma Marine Air Station.
48. The LDP and its coalition partners, the SDP, and the new party Sakigake reached agreement on the policy that would be followed on Okinawa when the Hashimoto cabinet was agreed upon. Specifically, the ruling coalition noted that U.S. forces in Japan were concentrated in Okinawa, and therefore, the government would promote a reduction and consolidation of these bases within the aims set forth under the bilateral U.S.-Japan security treaty. Attention was to be given to improving the SOFA implementation, and the governing parties agreed to make "strong efforts to produce visible results within the year" in response to Okinawa's demands through SACO and the Consultative Committee on U.S. Base Problems in Okinawa (Okinawa Beigun Kichi Mondai Kyōgikai).

U.S. bases in Okinawa.[49] But the U.S.-Japan response was not motivated simply by events in Okinawa. The two governments had been planning a major policy statement on the alliance, and working-level talks on efforts to expand the basis of bilateral cooperation in cases of regional crises had focused attention on the effort to reaffirm and redefine security cooperation after the cold war.[50] The Okinawa base protest constituted an unexpected setback for this process, and policymakers from both governments were anxious to ensure that it did not disrupt the broader goals of the alliance.[51]

The attention of Prime Minister Hashimoto, and the working-level consultations between the U.S. and Japanese policymakers, resulted in a U.S.-Japan agreement to return one of the most problematic bases, the Futenma Marine Air Station.[52] Hashimoto, accompanied by U.S. Ambassador to Japan Walter Mondale, announced on April 13, 1996 that Futenma—a key base in the Okinawa Prefecture's Base Reduction Action

49. The mandate of SACO also included consultations on how to better implement the terms of SOFA in an attempt to respond to the demands for revision as a result of the rape. The members of SACO included, on the Japanese government side, the director general of the North American Bureau (MOFA) and the director general of the DFAA (Defense Agency), and on the U.S. government side, the Deputy Assistant Secretary for East Asian Affairs (DOS) and the Deputy Assistant Secretary for Asia Pacific (DOD), and members of their respective staffs.

50. The two governments were discussing how to consider ways in which the U.S.-Japan alliance could be more effectively implemented in situations such as a crisis on the Korean peninsula. This effort, referred to as the drafting of "new guidelines" for U.S.-Japan security collaboration, was central to the bilateral security dialogue when Prime Minister Hashimoto took office.

51. Since the cabinet changed in January, the U.S. and Japanese governments had been working both through the SACO process and in behind-the-scenes conversations with Prime Minister Hashimoto and his advisors on plans for reducing the U.S. military presence in Okinawa. The U.S. side had begun to consider the possibility that the prime minister would ask for movement on the Okinawa bases, and both the U.S. ambassador in Tokyo and the Department of Defense staff began working on the possibility of returning Futenma Marine Air Station after Hashimoto and Clinton met in Santa Monica in February. See Funabashi Yōichi, *Dōmei hōryū* (Tokyo: Iwanami Shoten, 1997), chapter 6.

52. Located alongside the island's main commuter highway, and occupying about 45% of the city of Ginowan, it was a overwhelming symbol of the problems created by U.S. military bases in the densely populated central region of the Okinawa main island. The announcement took many by surprise. Senior officials in governments on both sides of the Pacific were not informed of the plan, and local military commanders in Okinawa were also unaware. According to the account by Funabashi Y(ichi, however, the governor of Okinawa was consulted by Prime Minister Hashimoto prior to the announcement of the Futenma Return. For a careful analysis of how the reorganization of Okinawa bases intersected with broader U.S. strategic thinking at the time, see Gabe Masaaki, "The Changing U.S.-Japan Alliance System: The Return of Futenma Marine Air Station and the New Guidelines," conference paper prepared for *Ryūkyū in the History of East-Asia, Asia, and the World*, 27th Conference of German-Speaking Orientalists, Bonn, Germany, September 30–October 2, 1998.

Program, would be returned within five to seven years. U.S. Marine aircraft and helicopters would be relocated to Iwakuni Air Base on Honshu and to other bases within Okinawa. The prime minister also announced that he intended to create a Task Force on Futenma, to assist in the process of considering the implications of reverting land to civilian use.[53] This was a visible response to the demands of the Okinawa prefectural government, and in a press conference that evening, Ōta stated that he saw it as a "demonstration of the government's sincerity" in response to the prefecture's needs.[54] Moreover, within days of the Futenma announcement, the Interim Report of the bilateral SACO was released.[55] A total of eleven facilities were earmarked for full or partial return by the U.S. military.

While the initial reaction in Okinawa was positive, there was a concern that the SACO process did not fully meet the demand for base reduction. Many of the facilities were to be returned with the proviso that replacement facilities be found elsewhere.[56] The prefecture's long-term desire for reduction and ultimate withdrawal of U.S. forces appeared to be compromised by a SACO focus on simply reducing the amount of land used by U.S. military forces. The decision to return facilities to civilian use were seen as conditional, since the proviso that U.S. forces on these bases would be relocated suggested that the Okinawan desire for a reduction in U.S. forces would be ignored. In fact, it was precisely this divergence of opinion that ultimately strained the relationship between Tokyo and Okinawa and frustrated efforts to negotiate a mutually acceptable policy on the U.S. bases. While Tokyo (as well as Washington) sought to consolidate existing forces, the Okinawa prefectural government looked to a reduction in overall U.S. military presence.

Implementing the Futenma agreement revealed how difficult it would be for the governor and prime minister to reach a compromise.[57]

53. This group, formally named the Task Force on ssues Related to the Futenma Return, was established on May 9, 1996.

54. Okinawa Taimusu, 50-nenme no gekido, 122.

55. See The SACO Interim Report, released April 15, 1996.

56. Previous experience with this sort of approach included the Naha Military Port, a facility in downtown Naha City that the prefecture and the city want to use for commercial development. While a plan to move the facility further north to Urasoe City has been developed, the mayor of Urasoe City has yet to approve the plan because of local protest.

57. Prime Minister Hashimoto appointed Okamoto Yukio as his special advisor on Okinawa. Okamoto was an independent consultant who had formerly been a career bureaucrat in the Ministry of Foreign Affairs. Throughout the negotiations between Governor Ota and Prime Minister Hashimoto, Okamoto acted as a personal envoy of the prime minister. He acted as a direct channel between the two in an effort to keep the dialogue from being captured by the various bureaucracies with stakes in the outcome of their deliberations.

After the announcement of Futenma's return in April 1996, the Ministry of Foreign Affairs and the Defense Agency spent months trying to identify possible sites for relocating the U.S. Marines. The most attractive option was to move Marine helicopters to Kadena Air Force Base, the largest U.S. military base on the island. Several sites on Kadena were considered suitable for constructing a heliport, but ultimately the Kadena consolidation plan was rejected. A variety of explanations have been cited. The first was that local political leaders opposed the idea, with the mayors of Kadena Town, Chattan Town, and Okinawa City—three of the four municipalities surrounding Kadena Air Force Base—issuing public statements that they would not accept the "buildup" of U.S. military operations there.[58] A second difficulty with the Kadena option was that the U.S. Air Force did not appear enthusiastic about sharing facilities with the Marines. Third, when Ōta met with U.S. Secretary of Defense William Perry, he argued that the environmental damage that would be created by building a heliport on Kadena was unacceptable. Finally, media reports indicated that the government was already contemplating a new type of installation, namely, an offshore base. It would reduce the impact on Okinawan communities and would allow the Marines to consolidate their forces on the northern part of the island.

As Tokyo policymakers explored the options for relocating the Marines, Governor Ōta sought to bolster his political resources prior to meeting with Prime Minister Hashimoto. The summer of 1996 was, in retrospect, the defining moment for Ōta and the prefectural government. In June, he visited Washington, D.C., and met with Defense Secretary Perry and his staff.[59] At this meeting, Ōta explained the strength of local protest against the bases, and he presented his arguments for reducing the U.S. military presence. It was the first time a Japanese governor had made a direct appeal to the U.S. government on the issue, and by moving outside the traditional diplomatic channels, Ōta impressed his local con-

58. Mayors of three municipalities formed a consultative committee (*renryaku kyōgi kaigi*) on September 16, 1996 in recognition of the need to form a concerted stance opposing the attempt to move forces from Futenma to Kadena.
59. On June 17, the governor and Secretary William Perry spent forty minutes reviewing the process of the SACO deliberations. While Governor Ōta conveyed his appreciation for the decision to return Futenma Marine Air Station, he noted that thirteen townships had passed resolutions against the construction of replacement facilities. He also argued that the environmental impact of building new facilities would be in violation of his administration's efforts to protect Okinawa's natural landscape. In subsequent discussions with staff, the governor focused on how bases intervened in the economic growth of the prefecture. Moreover, he stated that he had no opposition to the U.S.-Japan security relationship, but rather wanted the main islands of Japan to assume more of the burden for the basing of U.S. forces in Japan.

stituents with his ability to break through the "diplomatic wall" (*gaikō no kabe*) that had relegated Okinawa to the backburner of the alliance dialogue. On July 10, as the governor made his appearance in the Japanese Supreme Court. His testimony was televised throughout Japan.

But perhaps the most crucial event for Ōta was the much-anticipated prefectural referendum on the U.S. bases in Okinawa scheduled for September 9, 1996. The groundswell of popular opposition to the bases in the fall of 1995 and subsequent popular support for his confrontation with the central government in the courts convinced many of the governor's advisors that a more formal statement of the will of the Okinawa people was necessary. The president of the Okinawa Prefectural Federation of the Japanese Trade Union Confederation (Rengō Okinawa), Toguchi Masahiro, played a key role in organizing the referendum, assisted by academic advisors from the University of the Ryukyus who specialized in constitutional and administrative law.[60] According to Toguchi, the referendum would give the Okinawan people a voice in the policy-making process over the bases for the first time.[61] The provisions of the Local Autonomy Law required signatures of one-fiftieth of the eligible voters to request a governor to hold a referendum. On May 8, 1996, after a broad signature drive that mobilized members of Rengō Okinawa and other affiliated labor organizations, citizens' groups, and political party councils throughout the prefecture, Toguchi submitted the referendum petition to Ōta with 34,500 signatures. On May 20, the prefectural assembly was called to approve a referendum ordinance and a supplementary budget for its implementation. While conservative political parties were not in favor, with prefectural assembly elections coming up in early June they were hesitant to declare their opposition. Assembly deliberations on the referendum were postponed until after the election on June 12, when the progressive parties picked up two additional seats in the assembly.[62] Despite the LDP's argument that a referendum "went against parliamentary democracy,"[63] in an extraordinary session the assembly voted to go ahead with the proposed referendum by a vote of 26 to 17. Implementation headquarters was established within the governor's of-

---

60. Governor Ōta also indicated that he would convey the results of such a referendum to the U.S. and Japanese governments.

61. For a detailed analysis of the organization of the referendum and its results, see Robert D. Eldridge, "The 1996 Okinawa Referendum on U.S. Base Reductions: One Question, Several Answers," *Asian Survey* 37.10 (October 1997).

62. This was the first time since 1980 that the progressives enjoyed a majority in the prefectural assembly.

63. Eldridge, "The 1996 Okinawa Referendum," 888.

fice, and the months leading to the referendum in early September saw an array of contradictory sentiments within Okinawa over how Governor Ōta should proceed in his strategy of challenging the central government's policy over the bases. A number of groups called for a boycott of the referendum, and despite active—and in the eyes of some, rather interventionist—efforts by the prefectural government and other groups, the outcome of the vote was less enthusiastic than the proponents had hoped.[64] The voter turnout rate of 59.53% was lower than for the prefectural assembly elections held in June (66.4%); it was also below that of the last gubernatorial election in 1994 (62.5%). Moreover, the vagueness of the phrasing of the referendum, the option of only "agree" or "oppose," and the relatively large number of voters who left their ballot blank, made it difficult to interpret just how representative the results were of public opinion in Okinawa. Nonetheless, 89% of those who voted in the referendum responded that they wanted the bases reduced.

Consequently, Ōta began his deliberations with Hashimoto with a weaker demonstration of public opinion than he had hoped for. The Supreme Court had already ruled in favor of the central government, and while the SACO process addressed many of the governor's specific complaints against the U.S. military, the open and unresolved question of Futenma's relocation made the Ōta-Hashimoto dialogue key to the resolution of the base crisis. The governor and the prime minister met a total of seventeen times over the course of the next year, but they never directly addressed their key difference. Okinawa's governor wanted the number of U.S. military forces on his island reduced. Hashimoto offered base consolidation and greater national government engagement in assisting the prefecture to facilitate its long-term planning and development goals.

But Tokyo's assistance in implementing Okinawa Prefecture's "grand design" hinged on the prefectural government's accepting the consolidation of U.S. military bases on the island. By late 1996, it was also clear that Tokyo was proposing construction of a new base. Initial efforts to consolidate existing U.S. military facilities appeared unworkable. What emerged from extensive negotiations between Tokyo and Washington, between the various central bureaucracies and the prefecture, and between Ōta and Hashimoto was a proposal to build a sea-based heliport offshore. What is not clear is why this policy option became the sole option. Moreover, it is also not clear what role Okinawa's governor played in

64. For the reactions of the organizers, see Okinawa Taimusu, *50-nenme no gekido*, 166–74.

the development of this policy solution. The effort to address Okinawa base problems that began with the SACO deliberations ultimately ended in discord between Hashimoto and Ōta. Ōta never endorsed the heliport proposal publicly. Yet, he never publicly denounced it. Instead, he sat on the sidelines as Tokyo officials began to negotiate directly with the locality they had identified as the best site for relocating the Marines.

LOCAL POLITICIANS AND CITIZEN ACTIVISTS IN NAGO CITY

Local politics within Okinawa Prefecture grew far more complicated in the face of the national government's effort to relocate the Marines stationed on Futenma. Opinion was divided in the prefecture over Tokyo's "conditional" acceptance of a base return, but Tokyo had committed itself to the SACO agreement, and therefore to a resolution to the relocation problem.[65] The prime minister believed that he could count on the support of the governor and other local politicians to implement this compromise. By late 1996, however, it was obvious that local political leaders in Okinawa were in no position to cooperate with the national government on Futenma relocation. Citizens were already mobilizing to stop any attempt to accept new forces or new bases on the island.

When reports of the possibility of building a new base in the north surfaced in July 1996, the citizens of Nago City sensed that their community would become the object of Tokyo's attention, and they quickly organized a citizens' assembly. As a result, the mayor of Nago City, Higa Tetsuya, was asked to chair a new committee, one that opposed the new heliport. The first government statement about the proposal to build a new base for the U.S. Marines was made by Hashimoto during his visit to Okinawa. By November 1996, the head of the Japanese Defense Agency confirmed that Nago City was an attractive candidate for such a facility. This prompted a second citizens' assembly in Nago and adoption of a resolution against the new base. The SACO final report issued in December by the American and Japanese governments clearly indicated a new floating base would be built off the northeastern shore of Okinawa.

In spite of the prefectural government's efforts to transform the policy-making process, and to achieve a singular and unified Okinawan

---

65. While some aircraft were to be taken off the island, the problem for the Marine Corps was where to locate their helicopters, and the U.S. government argued that these helicopters had to remain close to the infantry units located at Camp Hansen in the northern part of Okinawa.

position on base reduction, Ōta remained strangely disengaged from the discussions with Nago. He continued to refuse to make any statement on his position on the sea-based heliport plan. Now the spotlight shifted to Nago City and to the reaction of Mayor Higa. The policy dialogue on the U.S. bases seemed to return to its old pattern, and once again the conversation was between the central government bureaucrats, the DFAA, and the head of local government. But the political consequences for Higa were quite different now than they had been prior to 1995. Cooperation with the national government, and particularly with the DFAA, was now viewed as complicity with Tokyo against the interests of Okinawan residents. More importantly, this was the first time since the end of World War II that Okinawans were asked to consider building a new base on their island. Higa was obliged, however, to consider the DFAA's request. He was formally confronted with Tokyo's policy choice in January 1997 when the director of the Naha office of the DFAA visited Nago to ask for the mayor's cooperation in conducting a preliminary survey of the coastal area under consideration. Higa refused, stating that he would not discuss the issue with DFAA without the presence of prefectural officials at any meeting.

But Ōta refused to acknowledge Higa's request or make any direct comment. Meanwhile, the vice-governor stated that it was up to the local community to decide whether to accept Tokyo's proposal. By April, as the prefectural government sat on the sidelines, Higa announced that he would permit a survey—with the proviso that it did not signify his acquiescence to Tokyo's policy. It was a temporizing step, and without the political support of Governor Ōta, undoubtedly Higa found himself in an increasingly difficult position. Moreover, officials in Tokyo had begun to hint at the considerable economic benefits to be gained were the residents of Nago to cooperate. The governor had to be consulted, however. Once the preliminary survey on the coast was complete, the DFAA was required to request permission from the prefectural government to conduct offshore boring tests. Officials in Naha announced in August that they would handle the request in a "procedural manner." Meanwhile, they would refrain from making a policy judgment.

Fearing that political leaders in Naha and Nago would succumb to pressure from Tokyo, local residents had already organized a Citizens' Referendum Promotion Committee. By the end of the summer, they had collected enough signatures for a local referendum in Nago City on the proposed heliport. They requested the local election committee to approve their call for a vote on the base relocation issue. In October, the Nago City assembly adopted an amended version of the referendum after Mayor

Higa himself added two additional responses to it. Instead of a clear "yes/no" vote, there were two conditional choices: a "yes" vote that indicated acceptance of the new base if there were to be economic advantages, and a conditional "no" that indicated rejection because of potential environmental damage. In other words, the wording of the referendum that was finally approved sought to address the possibility of public support if certain concessions were met—economic assistance and/or the protection of the environment.

With two months to go until the December 21 referendum, citizens mobilized on both sides of the issue. Tokyo worked hard to convince Nago residents to accept the heliport. Once the referendum was scheduled, the Citizens' Referendum Promotion Committee quickly transformed itself into the Committee against the Heliport Base. In the meantime, another citizens' group had organized themselves into the Nago City Economic Promotion Committee, which advocated acceptance of the new heliport on the condition that local economic development funds would be sufficiently attractive to residents. Throughout November, members of the Hashimoto cabinet visited Nago in an attempt to build local support for the new base. In early December, Tokyo announced a program of economic assistance for the entire northern region of Okinawa.[66] The DFAA held explanatory meetings on the heliport. DFAA officials also went door-to-door in Nago explaining to residents the economic benefits that would accrue should the base be constructed.

Like Ōta, Mayor Higa found it necessary, and perhaps even expedient, to comply with established administrative procedures at the same time that he denied acceptance of the policy option advanced by Tokyo. As it turned out, the December 1997 Nago City referendum yielded a majority (52%) against construction of the heliport. The mayor then an-

---

66. There were a number of projects identified with the package put together just prior to the local referendum vote in Nago. Some of what was reported as the Hokubu shinkōsaku package had been part of the effort to consult with local officials in 1997, and some was a continuation of funding for projects already underway in the north. The majority of new projects, however, focused on revitalization efforts for downtown Nago City, and thus the package was clearly seen as contingent on the Nago City government's acceptance of the heliport plan. Much of what was reported consisted of "preliminary studies" or "feasibility studies" on projects related to tourist facilities. Community service projects funded by the DFAA subsidy program included things such as a new swimming pool and other sports-related facilities, and a new women's center. It was clear that the items were hastily put together, and there was no overall vision for economic development for the north. See Okinawa Taimusu, ed., Mini to ketsudan—kaijo heripōto mondai to Nago shimin tōhyō (Naha: Okinawa Taimususha, 1998), 79–96 for a discussion of the economic package.

nounced that, while he was officially accepting the Tokyo proposal, he was also resigning as mayor of Nago City. In other words, he played his appointed role as national policy administrator, yet simultaneously acknowledged that he could not represent the citizens of Nago in good faith. Throughout all of this, observers in both Tokyo and Okinawa watched to see what stance the governor would take on the heliport. On February 7, 1998, two days before the new mayoral election in Nago, Ōta announced that he would reject any plan that involved relocating existing U.S. military facilities within Okinawa Prefecture. Two days later, the newly elected mayor of Nago City, Kishimoto Takeo, immediately followed suit and announced that he would abide by Ōta's decision.[67] Thus, Tokyo's endeavor to convince Nago to accept its new heliport proposal was defeated.

Tokyo's proposal to build a sea-based facility was rejected by the citizens of Nago and, subsequently, the governor. But Ōta's avoidance of the dialogue between the DFAA and Nago City, and the timing of his announcement to reject relocation within the prefecture, left many wondering about his role in the policy process. Had he compromised with Tokyo, or not? Why hadn't he rejected the relocation idea earlier? Why did he refuse to join deliberations between Higa and Tokyo? Ōta later claimed that he was not consulted by Tokyo on the heliport proposal, and insisted that he had informed Hashimoto and others that there were limits as to what the citizens of Okinawa would accept for the return of Futenma. His silence on the Nago relocation plan simply indicated his willingness to see if Tokyo could convince the residents of the merits of the plan.[68] Whatever Ōta's motivations, it is clear that the roles of national policy administrator and representative of citizen interest carried a different weight for Ōta and Higa. The extent of the division within Nago City was clear in the months leading up to the referendum, and while a numerical majority against the heliport carried the day, the election that followed produced a new mayor who was not openly opposed to Tokyo's proposal. The promise of economic rewards for Nago City was

---

67. Kishimoto Takeo worked for former Mayor Higa and was widely associated during the election with the group that advocated the need for economic stimulus for Nago City. Once elected, however, he saw the heliport proposal as an issue for the governor and Tokyo to resolve. Moreover, he pointed out that his victory in the election was not solely determined by his own stance on the base. His supporting coalition of Nago City voters, some of whom strongly opposed the heliport proposal, he argued, were people he had known for most of his life. Interview with Kishimoto Takeo, May 1998.

68. Governor Ōta himself has refused to comment on his thinking during this time, but he intends to tell his side of the story in a forthcoming book about his experience in coping with the base problem. Interview with Ōta Masahide, October 1998.

a significant factor in both the referendum and the election. Yet, if the referendum represented a defeat for the old bargain of money for bases, it also revealed the depth of division within the Nago community over Tokyo's proposal.

LOCAL POLITICS AND NATIONAL POLICY: THE CASE OF U.S. BASES IN OKINAWA

The need for "rationalizing" the functions of government have produced a number of changes in the legal basis upon which authority and obligation are shared by central and local governments in Japan. But it is not clear that there is room in Japanese politics for local politicians to take the initiative in policy-making if that initiative is in direct confrontation with the policies outlined by the national government.[69]

The efforts by the former governor of Okinawa, Ōta Masahide, to alter Tokyo's approach to the U.S. military bases on his island revealed how profoundly difficult it is for local governments to balance their executive task of administrative obligations to the center against the political task of advocating local citizen interests. While the early stages of Ōta's challenge to national authority appeared to produce greater access to decision making at the national level, the tasks of representing citizen interests and simultaneously accommodating Tokyo's aim to retain the U.S. military presence in Okinawa became untenable for the governor. Moreover, his attempt to gain greater legal clarity on these contradictory roles reinforced the notion that local officials are responsible first and foremost to Japan's national government and its interpretation of the public interest. The Supreme Court upheld the national government's interpretation that public interest being served by the bases was in fact the national public interest (*kokumin no kōeki*) in the face of Ōta's assertion of the interests of Okinawa's residents (*kenmin no kōeki*), but it made no direct comment on the underlying *political* question posed by Ōta about the role of local politicians in articulating the voice of their constituents in Japanese politics.

Perhaps no other issue in recent Japanese politics has severely pitted locally elected officials against the national government more than the U.S. base protest in Okinawa. For three years, the governor and his prefecture sought to change national policy, and in doing so, the gover-

---

69. See, for example, Kurt Steiner, Ellis S. Krauss, and Scott C. Flanagan, eds., *Political Opposition and Local Politics in Japan* (Princeton: Princeton University Press, 1980), and Steven R. Reed, *Japanese Prefectures and Policymaking* (Pittsburgh: University of Pittsburgh Press, 1986).

nor exploited a variety of political resources. By taking the policy confrontation with Tokyo to the courts, and in publicly charging the national government with neglect of Okinawa's citizens, Ōta drew attention to the legal, political, and economic complexities that surround Tokyo's policy of providing bases for the U.S. military in Japan. By framing the issue in terms of the national government's responsibility to its citizens, Ōta and others in Okinawa sought to break through the "diplomatic wall" that had protected the U.S.-Japan alliance from domestic criticism.

While in the final analysis Ōta was unsuccessful in changing national policy, his prefectural government successfully questioned the basic premise that informs the current policy-making process in Tokyo— namely, that national security provisions take precedent over local interests. The Supreme Court decision upheld this premise, but it did so based on a procedural argument that the Japanese government was obligated to fulfill its commitment to the U.S.-Japan security treaty. It did not argue outright that the national government had full authority over the making of national security policy. The Okinawa challenge brought to light several aspects of Japan's security and foreign policy that had long been ignored. First, the national government depends heavily on local government officials to maintain support for the U.S. military presence. Despite these claims that national security and foreign policy-making is solely and legitimately the prerogative of the national government, local governments are intimately involved in the implementation of Japan's security policy, particularly when it comes to the U.S. military presence in Japan.[70] Thus, while local governments and residents of local communities are excluded from the process that generates the policies, they are expected to cooperate in their implementation.[71] The efforts of the governor and other local politicians to represent Okinawan interests to Tokyo with regard to the bases, therefore, was interpreted by

70. In fact, postwar Japanese security planning has not been characterized by a centralized and authoritative role for the national government. Local governments have periodically resisted the national government's policy, on the basis that Japan's alliance with the U.S. in practice violates the spirit of Japan's constitution. For an analysis of how the national government had to reclaim its prerogative to make and implement security policy in the postwar period, see my forthcoming book *Negotiated Security: The Japanese State in the Cold War.*

71. The role of local government in implementing Japan's security cooperation with the U.S. is expected to increase under the legislation on the 1997 revised U.S.-Japan Defense Guidelines currently before the Japanese Diet. Use of civilian ports and airfields, as well as other types of cooperation with the U.S. and Japanese militaries by local authorities is expected to increase as U.S.-Japan cooperation in regional crises expands.

many in Tokyo as striking a blow against the authority of the national government in a policy area that the central government jealously guarded as its own.

Second, while there is a long history of conservative-progressive debate over the U.S.-Japan alliance, there has been little examination of the social impact of the presence of U.S. military forces in Japan. The concentration of U.S. forces in Okinawa Prefecture since the 1970s has removed this issue from the daily lives of most Japanese. Thus, the issues faced by Okinawans seem distant, both geographically and temporally, from those who live in Tokyo or other parts of the country. While at first glance the anti-base movement that reemerged in Okinawa in the 1990s seemed reminiscent of the old struggle between progressives and conservatives, a struggle that infused national debate at the time of the Anpō in the 1960s and the Okinawa reversion movement in the 1970s, there was a decidedly new political vocabulary that accompanied this recent protest against the U.S. bases in Okinawa.

Both Ōta's efforts to articulate a unitary prefectural position and citizen activism against the heliport in Nago City revealed that the recent citizen protest in Okinawa was directed at more than the U.S. military bases. It was not only a protest against a particular policy but also a demand for a new way of thinking about citizen representation in Japanese politics. The Women against Military Violence argued for a safer environment for women. The Citizens against the Heliport protested against the heliport not simply because it was a military base but also because it threatened the quality of life enjoyed by Nago's citizens. The Group to Protect Life (Inochi wo Mamorukai),[72] the group that represented those in the north who wanted to keep the government from building the base, pointed to the need to protect the coastal waters—and the manatees (jūgon) that visited there—and the environmental diversity of the northern mountain area (yanbaru). The alternative vision provided by these various groups within Okinawa suggested that concrete infrastructure and large construction projects were not the only means of thinking about Okinawa's future. The voices were multiple even if the aim, stopping the government from building the base, was singular. The rhetoric of the older, more established base protest groups may seem dated, but the language and actions of newer groups that came to the fore in the

---

72. This was a slogan used by the first leaders of the islandwide protest in the 1950s. Nuchido takara was the phrase then used. In standard Japanese, this means inochi koso takara, or "life is the greatest treasure."

1995 "islandwide protest" (*shimagurumi tōsō*) were imminently under-standable to Japanese across the country who wanted to see their governments, local and national, become more responsive to and reflective of citizen interests. Tokyo's insistence that U.S. military bases must continue to be concentrated within Okinawa Prefecture was seen, therefore, as a symbol of their government's willingness to ignore its own citizens.

Finally, the policy dilemmas faced by local governments as a result of the U.S. military bases in Okinawa are different in scale and in scope from those faced by other base communities in Japan. Other communities do share similar problems, most notably those with U.S. bases in Kanagawa Prefecture. Yet they do not persist to the same degree as in Okinawa, where administrative problems faced by local officials are complex and unique. While some common cause may be found with other local governments on the need to revise aspects of the SOFA, nonetheless, there are a host of issues associated with the base presence in Okinawa that are peculiar to individual bases and communities. More than anything else, land use and urban development laws will need to be specially crafted to cope with the reduction and consolidation of the U.S. military presence in the prefecture. Jobs, infrastructure, investment funds, and regional subsides are all influenced by the U.S. military presence on the island.

Unless parallel efforts to address the structural weaknesses—and dependence—of the Okinawa economy are undertaken, little can be done to change the economic interests that beggar the process of base reduction. The Okinawa prefectural government may have embraced such an approach when it linked a new long-term economic vision to a phased program of base reduction. But it may have put the cart before the horse in identifying base reduction as its top priority without first gaining Tokyo's cooperation for its new economic vision. Likewise, the national government may also have lost an opportunity to gain prefectural cooperation in its base consolidation efforts by ignoring the fact that it is responsible for the current structure of Okinawa's economy, and that it thereby holds the key to untangling the conflicting interests that make finding a way out of the current stalemate possible. Forcing the Nago City government's hand on the base relocation issue simply had the effect of repeating old mistakes, and reinforced the perception that Tokyo sees Okinawa only as a place to deposit U.S. military bases that are unwelcome in other parts of Japan.

Okinawa's challenge to Tokyo not only has obvious implications for Japanese security policy but also offers a clear example of how local governments may interpret and reinterpret the latitude afforded them by recent changes in the Local Autonomy Law.[73] The legal test of the intent of Japan's Local Autonomy Law provided a national stage from which Ōta could publicize the problems faced by Okinawans. It also elevated national consciousness about the debate over the administrative obligations of local political leaders. Closer to home, the Ōta government also sought to change the role played by the prefectural government in policy-making concerning the Okinawa bases. The policy of base reduction coupled with the Cosmopolitan City Formation Concept was ambitious, yet the rationale behind it paved the road for the prefecture to exercise greater discretion over the localities in Okinawa. Ōta's aim was to assert prefectural prerogatives in a policy-making process that had relied on the ability of the national administrative bureaucracy (in this case, the Defense Agency) to provide incentives to municipalities to accept the U.S. military presence. But the deliberations between Tokyo and Nago City reveal that Ōta misjudged the political dynamics within his own prefecture. By standing on the sidelines and allowing Mayor Higa to contend with Tokyo alone, Ōta hurt his standing among other local leaders in Okinawa badly. Indeed, he may have missed a golden opportunity to shape the dialogue with Tokyo. Simultaneously, he missed an opportunity to claim his mantle as the representative of Okinawa's citizenry. Citizen activism carried the day in Nago, while the prefectural government appeared indecisive and disengaged at precisely the moment when the governor's arguments on the U.S. bases most needed to be validated.

Today, Ōta Masahide no longer presides over the prefectural government, and his defeat in the November 1998 election is seen by many in Tokyo as a return to the less caustic, more cooperative relationship between the prefecture and the national government. Moreover, Governor Inamine's proposal to build a new joint civilian-military airport in the northern region of Okinawa signals his acceptance of the conditional nature of the Futenma return. Yet even he has put a fifteen-year limit on U.S. military access to the new airport. After his election Inamine announced that his first task was to reopen channels of communication with Tokyo. The following day Cabinet Secretary Nonaka stated his will-

---

73. The revision of the Local Autonomy Law in 1991 removed some of the strictures on local governments that challenged central policies, and the Law to Promote Decentralization that passed in 1995 promises to give greater latitude to localities in formulating and implementing local initiatives. The most significant change for the Okinawan base protest, however, was the removal of the provision allowing the central government to remove a governor from office if he disobeyed central authority from the Local Autonomy Law.

ingness to consider Inamine's proposal for relocating the U.S. Marines from Futenma. But the cabinet secretary also rejected putting a time limit on the use of the facility. Inamine's ability to negotiate Okinawan interests with Tokyo has yet to be demonstrated. His victory over Ōta suggests, however, that the majority of Okinawan voters were anxious to end the confrontation with Tokyo.

Citizens' groups are likely to continue to mobilize around the base issue, and opposition to the construction of a new base on the island is virtually guaranteed. Miyagi Yasuhiro, head of the Nago citizen group that halted the heliport option, has already announced that efforts to halt Inamine's proposed joint-use base in the north are already underway. Moreover, many of the administrative problems outlined by the Okinawa prefectural government continue to plague local communities. But it is clear that future governors will not be able to stop the land expropriation process as Ōta did. The political strength of the *hansen jinushi* and their supporters has been diminished by the 1997 Special Measures Law, by which the government's continued access to Okinawan land seems secure.[74] Still, if opinion polls are any indication, opinion in Okinawa on the base issue remains closer to the position advocated by Ōta.

The Okinawa base issue shows how governors, and other locally elected politicians, can derive bargaining strength from citizen activism, particularly against policies highly valued by the national political leadership. Because the U.S. bases were important to Tokyo, the inability of former Prime Minister Murayama to cope with the Okinawa protest resulted in his resignation. Hashimoto too needed a successful resolution on the Okinawa issue, and while his resignation was prompted by an electoral setback for the LDP in the Upper House elections, it was apparent that Ōta's refusal to cooperate in a compromise effort on the heliport was a blow to the LDP's prestige. For a time, Ōta gained Tokyo's attention, but his ultimate refusal to allow relocation of the U.S. facilities within the prefecture ended his negotiating credibility with both the politicians and the bureaucrats who had sought to find a middle ground.

The effort to translate the expression of local protest in Okinawa into a new national policy on the U.S. bases raises important questions about the demands placed on local politicians, both by Tokyo and by their constituents. If the recent protest against U.S. military bases in Okinawa

---

74. In 1998, the Prefectural Land Expropriation Committee did not approve recent Defense Agency requests for extensions on some base land, however. This suggests that there continues to be opposition to the procedural as well as the substantive position of the national government's land claims.

is any indication of these pressures, it seems that there is little room within the current structure of Japanese politics for local politicians to sustain opposition to Tokyo's policy priorities in a case where local citizen interests sharply diverge from the national policy agenda. Japan's Supreme Court did not rule in favor of local interests. Even more significantly, an overwhelming majority of the Diet passed a new law that insures that national government control over base lands will not be threatened in the future. And perhaps most important of all, the attempt to recast the balance of political bargaining power between the prefecture and the national government over long-term policy goals for Okinawa faltered as various economic interests splintered the singular vision that Ōta and Yoshimoto had advanced for Okinawa.

The politicians who played the leading roles in the negotiations in the Okinawa base protest—Prime Minister Hashimoto Ryūtarō, Governor Ōta Masahide, and Nago City Mayor Higa Tetsuya—have left office, but the base problem remains. Today, Prime Minister Obuchi, Governor Inamine Keiichi, and Mayor Kishimoto Tateo confront almost the same thorny issues as their predecessors. Tokyo insists that the implementation of the U.S.-Japan agreement to return Futenma Air Station is contingent upon relocation of U.S. Marines within Okinawa Prefecture. Meanwhile, Okinawa Prefecture remains dependent on national subsides for its economic sustenance, and those who work in Nago city hall must prepare for the day when the mayor will be asked again to accept a new base that many of his constituents oppose. As long as the policy solution devised by the national government continues to be the construction of a new U.S. military base in Okinawa, the fiscal and regulatory power of Tokyo will have to contend with the strength of local citizen activism. And stuck in the middle of the fray will be the men and women that Okinawans have elected to office—the very same local officials that Tokyo depends on to implement its policy.

Kan-Min Relations in Local Government

Patricia G. Steinhoff

The four case studies in this volume present an intriguing array of center-local relations, which is the theme they were intended to address. In the process, they also reveal several different patterns of relationships between government officials and citizens in contemporary Japan. In each case study, the relationship between local government officials and ordinary citizens becomes an essential part of the explanation.

Carol Gluck has shown how the traditional distinction between *kan* (bureaucrats or officials) and *min* (the people), widely considered to constitute the fundamental structure of Japanese politics, was adapted following the introduction of constitutional government in the late Meiji era.[1] In the traditional conception of their relationship, the *kan* possessed authority over and looked after the *min* on behalf of the emperor. The structure was strictly centrist and hierarchical, so that local level *kan* above the village or town level were simply administrative conduits under the direction of central authority. Although elected officials under the Meiji Constitution of 1889 were initially intended to be representatives of the *min*, they soon came to be seen as part of the *kan*. Even at the lowest level of local self-government, elected officials came to act like bureaucrats and to be perceived as *kan* rather than *min* by those subject to their authority.

Now, three emperors, one constitution, and a century later, these studies reveal four quite different relationships between *kan* and *min* at the local level. The patterns constitute a logical continuum, but one that does not have an imperative historical or evolutionary order, since they are all found in roughly contemporaneous studies of local government in Japan at the end of the twentieth century. There may also be other

1. Carol Gluck, *Japan's Modern Myths: Ideology in the Meiji Period* (Princeton: Princeton University Press, 1985).

contemporaneous patterns that do not appear in the four cases at hand. This essay will first examine the four patterns of local *kan-min* relations found in the case studies and trace their connection to relations between local government and the center. It will then review several factors that interacted with local *kan-min* relations to affect the outcomes in the four cases.

FOUR LOCAL PATTERNS

Kan *over* Min

Ted Gilman's study of efforts at economic revitalization in a de-industrialized coal community in Kyushu represents a classic kind of *kan-min* relation, in which the local *kan* stands vertically above the local *min*, guiding and supervising affairs on their behalf. Gilman shows us local government officials who act to improve the welfare of the local citizenry, under the hierarchical guidance of national government.

In order to alleviate the local problems caused by the decline of the once-dominant coal industry in Omuta, the local officials look primarily to the center for funding. They study the economic development incentives offered by national government agencies and try to tailor local needs to fit the available national programs. Success is measured by the ability of local government officials to obtain national funding, which means that the policy priorities dictated by the center profoundly shape the local response. Gilman focuses on the efforts of a reform mayor whose primary credential is that instead of being a Mitsui man out of the coal industry elite, he is a local boy who made it into the ranks of the national bureaucracy and therefore knows his way around the government offices of Tokyo.

Despite Omuta's history as the site of a massive union dispute from 1953–60, and therefore a place with a strong tradition of activism, the citizen input into the redevelopment efforts of the 1980s and 1990s was remarkably passive and unorganized. There were two basic channels for citizen input, and local government officials managed both of them vertically. One was the official panel of representatives of local organizations that served in an advisory capacity. Actually there were two advisory panels, because the main one representing the recognized social units in the community was all-male, so the women formed their own separate one. These two bodies presumably represented various social and economic constituencies in the community and thus were intended to provide formal channels for citizen input into the planning process. Gilman suggests that both of these advisory panels simply contributed general ideas to reports that ended up being organized, written, and ultimately ignored by local government officials.

The second form of citizen participation was through that chronically misused instrument of social science research, the questionnaire survey. The Omuta city government dutifully commissioned two surveys in 1984 and 1990 in order to find out what the community wanted. A professional survey research firm from elsewhere in Kyushu, apparently with considerable experience in local economic development projects, conducted both surveys using standard professional sampling procedures. The surveys presented respondents with fixed lists of potential economic development project areas that roughly corresponded to available sources of central government funding. The job of the citizen respondents in the sample was to rank their preferences from the list. The people who commissioned and administered the surveys thus controlled the range and quality of the input from anonymously and randomly selected citizens.

Interestingly, Gilman describes another survey conducted in 1986 by a local business organization. This survey asked open-ended questions about what kinds of improvements the respondents would like to see in their community, and it produced a rather different list of priorities, including items that were not even on the list in the other two closed-question surveys.

The overall pattern of *kan* over *min* is clear: local government, standing in a hierarchical relationship between the national government above and the citizens below, solicits formal (*tatemae*) input from the citizenry in order to make more appropriate selections on their behalf from the centrally determined policy menu. The citizens may appear to be the honored guests for whom the mayor serves as the head waiter, but the guests will in fact be served whatever the cooks in Tokyo have put on the menu, and then only until the daily special runs out.

Kan *Parallels* Min

Katherine Tegtmeyer Pak's study of the relations between local government and local private organizations in meeting the needs of foreign workers depicts a quite different relationship between *kan* and *min*, as well as between the center and local government. In this case the *kan* and *min* at the local level operate on parallel but separate tracks with some degree of common purpose.

The foreign worker "problem" is a product of Japan's economic boom of the late 1980s, which brought workers from less developed countries in Asia and the Middle East flocking to Japan to take the unskilled jobs that highly educated Japanese workers disdain. The Japanese government responded with a few modest programs for certain special categories of foreign workers. However, large numbers of foreigners who do not fit into these categories come on tourist or student visas and then work illegally, overstaying their visas and forming an easily exploited informal economy at the bottom of Japanese society. Both local government and local citizens' organizations serve as buffers between the foreign workers in local communities who are struggling with a range of personal problems, and the national government whose strict exclusionary policies are the source of at least some of those problems. However, the different structural positions of the local *kan* and *min* affect the kinds of support they can offer and to whom.

Local government dispenses various forms of government-funded assistance, but national government immigration policies constrain local officials to limit these services to legal immigrants with proper visa status. Private citizens' organizations have fewer resources, but they can serve as advocates and provide personalized support services for the illegal immigrants who are the most severely disadvantaged members of the local community. The resulting lineup is not the vertical pattern of Gilman's coal town, but rather a more functional, horizontal division of labor between local government and local citizens' groups who can meet different needs of the foreign workers in their community.

Not only is the relation between local government and local citizens not vertical; both the local *kan* and local *min* stand in a somewhat more independent and less passive position vis-à-vis the national *kan*. Although local government is formally obliged to report illegal immigrants and to deny them services, Tegtmeyer Pak points to examples in which sympathetic local officials work around these constraints creatively to offer services, or quietly fail to report illegal immigrants. The local citizens' groups express considerably stronger opposition to national government policies toward foreign workers, usually as part of their broader political disaffection.

These and other differences of status and perspective also help to explain why the local *kan* and local *min* are only occasionally able to work together in pursuit of their common purpose. Tegtmeyer Pak's image of parallel tracks heading in the same direction aptly captures this relationship between *kan* and *min* at the local level, because many factors still keep the two groups a measured distance apart, yet linked together by their common aims.

Min *Checks* Kan *as Equals*

Maclachlan's case study of information disclosure laws presents a more democratic model of the relationship between citizens and local officials. In this version the *min* hold the *kan* accountable for their actions and seek to make those actions more visible. The *min* therefore "checks" the *kan* in both senses of the word: the citizens assert the right to know what officials are doing, to check up on them, but they also use information disclosure to check or place limits on official excesses.

Information disclosure laws are a relatively recent phenomenon in Japan, with roots in local consumer movements. Maclachlan documents that they initially appeared at the local city level and then were adopted by prefectures as the idea spread. After many years of indecision, the Diet in 1999 enacted such a law at the national level. This activity not only has bubbled up from local initiatives to the national level but also is quite clearly the achievement of well-organized local citizens' groups who worked to get the laws passed. Particularly noteworthy is the coordinated effort by local citizens' groups in various communities to exercise the new information disclosure procedures in order to test compliance and, in the process, to reveal official misbehavior. Ironically, much of the overspending arises from local officials wining and dining national officials, ostensibly to cultivate support for local projects.

An oversimplified version of this story might read as a triumph of *min* over *kan* and local government leading national policy, but Maclachlan presents a much more complex and dynamic picture of these interactions. Although organized local citizens managed to get information disclosure laws enacted, the laws are rather limited and still permit considerable bureaucratic discretion and secrecy. Hence the pattern is not yet *min* over *kan*, but rather a more horizontal relationship in which *min* assert their equality with the local *kan* but are still trying to strengthen their hand.

Maclachlan depicts vividly the way both the original passage of information disclosure laws and their subsequent revision have spread laterally between communities and vertically between the local, prefectural, and national levels of government. The influences go in all directions, with no sense of the center leading or dictating to local government. Hence the assertion of equality between *min* and *kan* at the local level seems simultaneously to reduce the hierarchy between central and local government and to create new links between citizens in different communities, thereby opening channels for communication and influence to flow in all directions. Equality is by definition universalistic; once established, it tends to erode its boundaries.

Kan *Represents* Min

Smith's case study of the Okinawa base problem seems at first glance most notable for its confrontational center-local relations. The base problem had been festering for decades as the national government negotiated base arrangements with the United States while ignoring strong and well-organized protests at the local level. Governor Ōta suddenly thrust the local voice onto the national and international stage by refusing to cooperate with the standard national arrangement for overriding local resistance to the periodic renewal of private landholders' leases for base land.

A closer look at the nature of *kan* and *min* relations at the local level in this case reveals that the pattern is local *kan* representing local *min*. Governor Ōta grounded his unprecedented opposition to the center by characterizing himself as the elected representative of local interests rather than as the conduit to enforce national authority over the local citizenry. The conflict came to a head precisely at the point where the elected representative of the people of Okinawa was required by law to act as representative of the central government and violate the wishes of his constituents by signing the leases that the landowners had refused to sign. Ōta's dramatic move pushed Tokyo and Washington to negotiate the early return of some base land in Okinawa. Emboldened by the governor's stance and supported by his own local referendum, the mayor of Nago similarly represented his constituents by rejecting the central government's compromise solution of building a new offshore heliport adjacent to the town in order to permit the return of base land elsewhere in the prefecture.

The thrust of these actions was to try to assert the power of *min* over *kan*, even though the key players were themselves local officials. At the local level this initially produced enthusiastic support for elected officials who were willing to express strong citizen sentiments through bold confrontational politics. However, while it is deeply local in its impact, the base problem is intrinsically both national and international. The central government's response to Okinawa's continued resistance on the base issue was to turn off the tap on economic support to the prefecture. The issue remains unresolved and public sentiment about it in Okinawa has not changed. But in the face of heavy-handed economic reprisals from Tokyo, in the fall 1998 election the local *min* shifted their support to the gubernatorial candidate who proposed to represent them cooperatively rather than confrontationally to restore the flow of funds from the center. The local *kan*, even in very close collaboration with the local *min*, could not withstand the power of the center, and could not supplant the central government in negotiations with Washington.

Associations of Local Kan-Min *Patterns with Center-Local Relations*

These fascinating case studies have revealed four different patterns of *min* and *kan* relations at the local level that seem to be linked to distinctive relations between local and national government. With just four cases it is not possible to establish whether a particular pattern of local *kan-min* relations is necessarily associated with a particular type of center-local government relations. It may be useful, though, to summarize the associations found in the four cases as potential hypotheses for further investigation.

The classic *kan* over *min* pattern at the local level is associated with dominance by the center over relatively weak local government initiatives. The pattern of *kan* parallel to *min* at the local level is associated with local government taking a somewhat more independent stance vis-à-vis national government. The pattern of *min* checking *kan* as equals is associated with a multi-directional flow of influence between local governments and the center, as well as between local governments in different places. And finally, the pattern of *kan* representing *min* at the local level is associated with resistance and confrontation by local government against national government. These associations suggest some potentially fruitful lines of inquiry with a wider selection of cases. A related set of questions concerns the relative effectiveness of the strategies that the local *kan-min* patterns generated in these particular cases.

STRATEGIES FOR LOCAL-CENTER RELATIONS

Three additional factors are present to varying degrees in the four cases: the mobilization and organization of local citizens; use of political opportunity; and use of the courts. These factors can be characterized as elements of the strategy through which the local *kan* and *min* pursued their goals. The outcome of each case is problematic, and the authors have been quite circumspect in their evaluations, so it is difficult to make an overall judgment about their relative success overall. Each case has had some successes and some failures, and they all represent dynamic situations changing in real time that may yet have different outcomes in the future. Hence the issue here is not to evaluate the strategies in terms of a clear outcome measure of the success of the case itself, but rather to see which cases have been able to use particular strategies more effectively than others, and why.

Nature of Citizen Activism

The four cases vary in the nature and structure of local citizen activism. That in turn is closely related to the nature of each issue and how amenable it is to solution at the local level. Rather than considering local activism in the abstract, therefore, it seems most appropriate to evaluate its nature and strength in the context of the particular issue and its potential for mobilizing an organized response from citizens.

The least active citizenry is certainly in Omuta, where formal organizational representation on advisory panels and anonymous sample surveys provided the major means of communicating with local government about development priorities. Omuta experienced very powerful and confrontational labor activism in the Miike mine up to 1960. That tradition of activism has been broken and dispersed by mine closures and de-population. The people who were left in Omuta have played a much more passive role in the redevelopment activities of the 1980s and 1990s.

While it is tempting to conclude that the absence of local citizen activism contributed to the weakness of Omuta's development efforts, it may also be that a general economic development initiative for a declining coal town is by its very nature less likely to inspire local activism than other issues. The only natural constituency for development per se would be local businessmen and landowners. The discrepancy between even the weakly expressed preferences of local citizens and the national development funding options that the city was able to pursue suggests that any greater citizen activism might have divided the community. Passivity thus might well have been the preferred alternative to overt conflict, rather than simply reflecting the absence or weakness of a desire for active community involvement.

All of the other three cases involve the active participation of organized citizens' groups with a particular commitment to the central issue of the case. The cases differ in their degree of mobilization, and in the parts of the community from which the activists are drawn. Even in these cases, however, the greatest amount of mobilization does not necessarily translate into the greatest success in achieving local goals, because of the nature of those goals. Some issues are simply more amenable to resolution through local action than others.

Citizens in Okinawa are the most heavily and broadly mobilized because of the long-festering nature of the base issue and its pervasive impact on the life of the prefecture. While there are certainly some internal conflicts of interest over the bases, there are a variety of organizations specifically devoted to opposing the bases, and many other general political and social organizations at the local and prefectural level have taken a position on the base issue. That sentiment was channeled into the election of Ōta as governor, and was also focused on a series of specific issue campaigns. Community activism subsequently focused on the prefecturewide referendum on the base issue and the smaller scale local referendum on the heliport in Nago.

The political channeling of anti-base sentiment contributed directly to the construction of the pattern of local *kan* representing *min* that generated a politics of confrontation with the center. The anti-base movement in Okinawa invokes historical legacies and is able to arouse some guilt in both Tokyo and Washington. Yet despite its initial successes, so far it has not proven to be strong enough to override the interests and power of the center. The crux of the problem is that this is simply not an issue that can be solved by local initiative alone. And while Okinawa's base problem attracts some sympathy outside of the prefecture, it is also not an issue on which citizen activism in other parts of Japan can be mobilized effectively to put additional pressure on the center. The issue attracts widespread and well-placed support within Okinawa, but elsewhere it is a relatively remote issue that draws its support from more marginalized political groups.

The problem of the locus of organized support also figures heavily in citizen activism on the foreign worker issue. In the communities that Tegtmeyer Pak studied there are local citizens' organizations working actively on behalf of the foreign workers, but the cause is unpopular with the general public, and the activists often have a history of involvement in other marginalized issues. As in the Okinawan base issue, foreign workers' problems cannot be resolved completely by citizen action at the local level because the issue is intimately tied to national government policies toward specific categories of foreign workers. The local citizens' groups that are interested in the problem do not have the numerical strength or social position to press for more general legal and social changes in the system itself that might alleviate the difficulties faced by foreign workers, even at the local government level. Thus the citizens' groups involved in this issue can work most effectively as personal support groups that help individual workers resolve their problems on a case by case basis.

The most effective citizen mobilization has been that of the information disclosure movement. In this case, local citizens who were not marginalized from the outset were able to form good coalitions and mount local campaigns to pass new information disclosure laws. Once the laws were in place, the same citizens' groups kept up the pressure by actively using them, among other things to reveal official misbehavior. The results of these information disclosures in turn reinforced citizen support for even stronger information disclosure laws at all levels of government.

This issue is not likely to pit major segments of the community against each other. The main opposition to information disclosure comes from bureaucrats, and some elected officials, who do not want their own behavior to come under public scrutiny. It is a relatively easy concept to sell to the voters and to local legislative bodies, but it has also turned out to have remarkable ramifications for the very structure of Japanese politics. In a sense, information disclosure constitutes the very essence of a more egalitarian relationship between *kan* and *min* in which the *min* both asserts and exercises the right to check the *kan*.

The information disclosure movement case also demonstrates how loosely linked local organizations can coordinate local actions, such as requests for certain kinds of information, and use them to produce a national impact when the combined results are reported in national mass media. As in the Okinawa base case, organized local community activism has been channeled effectively into local politics. The difference, however, is that in the information disclosure case much of the problem could be resolved by local action alone, and that action in turn has had a powerful cumulative demonstration effect that rippled upward and outward to replicate the success in other places.

Political Opportunity

The concept of political opportunity refers to changes in external political conditions that affect the capacity of social movements to mobilize support at different times, even though the issues they address may be chronic. The concept applies most directly to the Okinawan base movement, in which a particularly egregious crime by American military personnel against an Okinawan civilian child helped to channel long-standing grievances about the bases into an internationally visible social movement demanding immediate attention. The incident did not create the anti-base movement and the one-*tsubo* landowners' movement as an anti-base strategy, both of which already existed. Nor did it elect Ōta, who was already governor. What it did do was inflame local sentiment sufficiently to provide an opening for more dramatically confrontational politics between the prefecture and the center over the renewal of base leases, based on Governor Ōta's new construction of local *kan* as representing local *min*.

In both the Okinawa case and the information disclosure case, local activists also capitalized on the political opportunity created by changes in the makeup of national government in the early 1990s. In both cases local actors pushed their causes hard when the fall of the Liberal Democratic Party from power and the creation of a coalition government improbably headed by a Socialist Party (now renamed Social Democratic Party) leader made the center most sympathetic and vulnerable to these particular issues. The information disclosure activists were able to get visible support from reformist national leaders who personally promoted their cause sufficiently to produce legislation to be introduced into the Diet.

The political opportunity for the Okinawa case was more a question of finding a moment of vulnerability that weakened the negative response of the center. Ōta's refusal to sign the base leases was a much more difficult confrontation for Socialist Prime Minister Murayama than for any LDP prime minister before or since, and it did set in motion more active international negotiations to address the local concerns. Unfortunately, the window of opportunity soon closed on the Okinawa case. It remained open longer in the information disclosure case in the sense that prominent Diet members still supported the legislation, but it was shunted aside for a time by more pressing economic issues.

By contrast, neither the Omuta redevelopment nor foreign worker cases were able to take advantage of a favorable political opportunity. Both are social problems with specific and relatively recent histories, but nothing happened during the time periods studied to change the terms of their resolution.

In addition to lacking a mobilized and active citizenry, economic redevelopment in Omuta seems to have been chronically a little too late to succeed. Most of Omuta's local development initiatives were copied from ideas that had worked for other places applying for the same sources of funding. The political opportunity created by national legislation that provided special project funding for areas of declining industry had been lost by the time Omuta was ready to seek such support. In addition,

Omuta officials faced the additional burden of trying to prove that their copycat projects could be successful in competition with others that had gotten underway sooner.

There also does not seem to have been any political opening to change the conditions for the support of foreign workers during the period under study. Local government and local support groups were slow in developing more effective ways to deal with chronic problems, but the only thing resembling a political opportunity was the negative factor that Japan's own post-bubble economic difficulties had slowed the influx of new foreign workers and perhaps caused some others to go home. At a slightly earlier time than this case study documents, it is possible that the national government's creation of new special categories of legal foreign workers helped to engage local government in providing services to those workers. This may have expanded the sensitivity of the local *kan* to the problems of foreign workers and encouraged some creativity in occasionally extending services even to illegal workers. During the period of the study, however, there does not seem to have been any dramatic opening of political opportunity.

The concept of political opportunity can be useful in explaining why some social movements suddenly burst into action while others slog along at a slower pace. In this array of four cases, it does help to explain why the Okinawa base movement and information disclosure movement suddenly blossomed while the other two did not. It remains a very partial explanation, however, which simply can add extra weight to more basic internal factors such as the nature of the issue and the kind of citizen activism that has developed in each case.

Use of the Courts

The same two cases that utilized political opportunity effectively have also made creative use of the courts to press their claims. There is no intrinsic connection between these factors, since whether or not an issue can be taken to the courts depends on the nature of the claims that can be made, as much as on the willingness of local actors to press those claims in court.

In this array of four cases there does not seem to be anything about economic redevelopment in Omuta that might lend itself to a legal battle. There may be individual cases in which foreign workers' claims can be taken to court, but given the tenuous legal status of the workers, this does not appear to be a promising general strategy. In fact, one area of informal mutual cooperation between local government and local citizens' organizations assisting foreign workers is in resolving disputes with landlords and employers that cannot easily be taken to court. By contrast, in both the Okinawa case and the information disclosure case, key actors have made dramatic and creative use of the courts.

In the Okinawa case, by refusing to sign the base leases, Governor Ōta invited prosecution so that he could test the constitutionality of the law that required him to act as the representative of the national government on this matter. The Supreme Court ultimately sided with the national government and rejected Ōta's argument that as representative of his constituents he should not be forced to represent the national government against them. Yet by framing the issue as a constitutional challenge the governor bought valuable time and dramatically raised national and international awareness of the Okinawa base issue.

In the information access movement, local citizens' groups have used the courts to sue for disclosure of information under the new laws when bureaucrats have rejected their requests. It is particularly notable that these laws explicitly incorporate the possibility of using the courts to force disclosure, in addition to providing for local panels to which the refusal to disclose information can be appealed. Although petitioners do not always win in court, the fact that they can go to court, and that they often do win, changes the terms of decision making for local officials who must respond to disclosure requests. For this reason, the requirement in the draft national information disclosure legislation that cases had to be filed in Tokyo District Court came under fire for making court access too difficult for people who are not based in Tokyo. In the final version of the legislation, cases can be filed in eight district courts, with provision for others to be added later. This change in itself reflects a shift in the center-local balance of power and carries the potential of promoting more local initiative through the courts in the future.

The information disclosure case also tests the limits of Frank Upham's theory that when major social issues are resolved through the courts in postwar Japan, the solution usually creates a mechanism for dispute resolution in which the bureaucracy retains control over the process and discretion in deciding outcomes.[2] The fact that information disclosure laws explicitly permit requesters to take their claims to court suggests that the framers of these laws have deliberately tried to get the matter out of bureaucratic hands. Since the disputes are necessarily about bureaucratic discretion, this may seem like an obvious provision. Yet in

2. Frank Upham, *Law and Social Change in Postwar Japan* (Cambridge: Harvard University Press, 1987).

the broader context of postwar Japanese law it is rather novel because it does not allow the court to hand the problem back to the bureaucracy.

The old stereotype that Japan is not a litigious society has long been undermined by careful empirical work demonstrating that there are serious structural barriers to litigation because of the limited number of judges carrying very heavy case loads.[3] Under these circumstances, when the results are predictable, it makes more sense to settle out of court for the prevailing rate that the court would award. However, individuals with social and political support behind them are increasingly willing to sue in order to claim or establish rights, particularly in issues that pit *min* against *kan.*

These two cases illustrate quite different ways of using the courts to pursue a social issue or establish rights. In one case, in a direct confrontation with the center, a key figure invited prosecution by defying a law in order to test its constitutionality. In the other, local citizens used the local courts to press claims against local bureaucrats. As cases like these are publicized and as more people become familiar with such uses of the courts, we can expect these strategies to be used more readily to settle disputes between a more equalized *min* and *kan.*

FINAL OBSERVATIONS

All four of these richly detailed case studies demonstrate the value of conducting case study research, whether of a particular community or a specific social movement. It is because their authors have spent extensive time in the field studying documents, asking questions, following events, and trying to understand these situations in context that we as readers can learn so much from them. The juxtaposition of the four cases enables us to see more clearly the factors that shaped them and affected their outcomes. Because the cases are so well developed and carefully presented we can find patterns through comparison that go beyond what the individual authors originally had to say about their single cases. Yet we could not readily find those patterns, and we certainly could not explore them in any detail, without the in-depth research provided in the individual case studies.

Through these cases we have been able to see not only a variety of forms of center-local relations, but the patterns of relationships be-

3. See John Owen Haley, "The Myth of the Reluctant Litigant," *Journal of Japanese Studies* 4.2 (summer 1978): 359–90, and J. Mark Ramseyer, "Reluctant Litigant Revisited: Rationality and Disputes in Japan," *Journal of Japanese Studies* 14.1 (winter 1988): 111–23.

tween local citizens and local officials, the *min* and the *kan*, that under-lie them. While these patterns are intriguing in and of themselves, they become even more useful when we can connect them to the use of different strategies either for resolving particular problems or for managing center-local government relations. Precisely because the cases narrate complex processes instead of presenting simplified formulas, we have been able to subject those processes to further comparative analysis.

With just four cases we can only advance some ideas and suggestions about these intricate relationships, but our findings here may inspire others to add their own cases to the comparisons, and to further extend and test these connections. Perhaps most importantly, the cases themselves are now available for further examination and they await further discoveries by other readers.

Contributors

THEODORE J. GILMAN is an assistant professor of political science at Union College in Schenectady, New York, and has been a visiting assistant professor at Kyūshū University. He has written *No Miracles Here: Fighting Urban Decline in Japan and the United States* (SUNY, forthcoming) and is currently studying regional political and economic ties in Northeast Asia. He received his Ph.D. from The University of Michigan.

Ellis S. Krauss is a professor at the Graduate School of International Relations and Pacific Studies, University of California, San Diego, and specializes in Japanese politics and policy-making and U.S.-Japan relations. He is the author of *Broadcasting Politics in Japan: NHK and Television News* (Cornell, forthcoming) and the author or editor of several other books, including *Political Opposition and Local Politics in Japan* (edited with Kurt Steiner and Scott C. Flanagan, Princeton, 1982).

PATRICIA L. MACLACHLAN is an assistant professor of Asian studies and adjunct professor of government at the University of Texas at Austin. She is the author of a forthcoming book entitled *Turned Away at the Gate?: The Politics of Postwar Japanese Consumerism*, as well as several articles on Japanese consumer-related issues.

SHEILA A. SMITH is an assistant professor in the Department of International Relations at Boston University. She was a Visiting Fellow at the University of the Ryukyus in 1998 and Visiting Associate Professor at the International Institute for Japanese Studies in 1999. Currently she is completing a manuscript on Japanese security planning entitled *Negotiated Security: The Japanese State in the Cold War.*

PATRICIA G. STEINHOFF is professor of sociology at the University of Hawaii and was founding director of the university's Center for Japanese Studies. She is the author of several books on conflict and social movements of the Left in pre- and postwar Japan, including, most recently, *Rengō Sekigun to Aum Shinrikyō: Nihon Shakai o Kataru* (with Itō Yoshinori; Sairyūsha, 1995), as well as numerous articles.

KATHERINE TEGTMEYER PAK is an assistant professor of political science at the New College of the University of South Florida. Currently she is completing a book that explains Japanese immigration policy through institutional and cultural analysis, and researching local responses to immigration in the advanced industrial democracies.

Index